Jake Rowley is a barrister at Farrar's Building specialising in high value and complex personal injury litigation. He has extensive experience of proceedings arising out of road traffic accidents and claims involving allegations of LVI.

He is well versed in the applicable legal principles relating to LVI cases as well as the varying forms of evidence regularly encountered in such claims including forensic engineering evidence dealing with damage consistency and/or occupancy displacement; expert medical evidence; insurer's CUE database searches; and social media evidence. Jake is known for his meticulous and forensic approach to considering the available evidence in LVI cases, which enables him to settle robust pleadings and give sensible and pragmatic advice on tactics and prospects of success in advance of trial. He prides himself on conducting thorough and robust cross-examinations of witnesses at trial. Jake's LVI practice is complemented by his significant experience of cases involving allegations of fraud/fundamental dishonesty.

Jake is instructed on behalf of the UK's biggest and most well-known motor insurers and is regularly invited to speak or provide training in this area to both solicitors and insurers.

This is Jake's second book published by Law Brief Publishing. His first book, *"Fundamental Dishonesty and QOCS in in Personal Injury Proceedings: Law and Practice"*, is also available.

Low Velocity Impacts in Road Traffic Accidents: Law and Practice

Low Velocity Impacts in Road Traffic Accidents: Law and Practice

Jake Rowley

Barrister

Farrar's Building, Temple

Law Brief Publishing

Published 2023 by Law Brief Publishing, an imprint of Law Brief Publishing Ltd
30 The Parks
Minehead
Somerset
TA24 8BT

www.lawbriefpublishing.com

Paperback: 978-1-914608-11-7

PREFACE

The overwhelming likelihood is that at some stage (particularly in the early years of practice), every personal injury practitioner, whether representing Claimants or Defendants, will be exposed to road traffic accident litigation. For those involved with such claims, having to deal with low-velocity impact cases is an inevitability. It is therefore critically important that all practitioners are aware of the legal framework applicable to such cases; the procedural steps required by them (or their opponents) to properly advance defences based on allegations of low-velocity impact; can spot the tell-tale signs of a low-velocity case early on; understand the types of evidence that are most frequently encountered in low-velocity impact cases, so that they know when to obtain such evidence, and how to best use it to their advantage; and have an appreciation of how such cases are adjudicated by the Courts and why (at least ordinarily) they succeed or fail at trial. This publication hopes to answer those questions and provide practical guidance on low-velocity impact cases, generally, from both Claimant and Defendant perspectives.

My thanks go to my publishers for entrusting me with the creation of this work; to my colleagues and clerks at Farrar's Building for their continued support and friendship; to my wonderful mother for her endless encouragement and unwavering confidence in me; and to Sinead for her boundless patience, constancy, and love. You have all played a part in the completion of this publication.

The law as stated is considered to be correct, and accurate, as at the 12th December 2022. Any errors are entirely mine.

Jake Rowley
December 2022

CONTENTS

CHAPTER ONE

WHAT IS A LOW VELOCITY IMPACT CLAIM?

What is meant when we refer to a 'low velocity impact[1]' claim (or 'LVI' for short)?

Such terminology is used in conjunction with claims arising out of a road traffic accident ('RTA') in which a Defendant alleges that the collision was so minor or insignificant in its nature that it was *incapable* of causing any occupant(s) of the vehicle any injury whatsoever or, often asserted in the alternative, that the nature of the collision was such that it was *inherently unlikely* that any occupant(s) of the vehicle did, in fact, sustain any injury.

Legally speaking, a defence which asserts that the collision was a low-velocity impact is a challenge to the *causation* of injury.

The issue arises most commonly (although by no means exclusively) in claims in which it is alleged that the Claimant sustained soft-tissue/whiplash type injuries to the neck, shoulder(s) and/or back. Given the prevalence of such injuries in LVI type cases it is in relation to these sorts of injuries that this publication focuses its attention, however the observations made apply equally to any injury which might have been allegedly suffered in a LVI type collision.

It is generally accepted that in order for an occupant of a vehicle to sustain soft-tissue/whiplash type injuries to their neck/shoulder(s) and/or back

---

[1] Sometimes also referred to as a 'low speed impact' or 'LSI' (for short) [although such description is, probably, inaccurate given the concern is with the forces transmitted as between the two vehicles, and not simply the speed that one/other/both are moving at]

they must experience a degree of occupant displacement within the vehicle in which they are travelling i.e. that is to say that their body must be physically moved/jolted by the impact caused by the Defendant's vehicle.

In simple terms, a LVI defence is one in which the Defendant argues that the circumstance of the collision, together with any other evidence which may have been collated, collectively demonstrate or tend to suggest that the forces transmitted between the Defendant's vehicle and the Claimant's vehicle, at the point of collision, were insufficient to cause occupant displacement or, as a matter of fact, did not cause such occupant displacement, and thus, the collision was incapable of causing any injury. This impartation of force is often referred to in the relevant authorities and elsewhere as the 'v' (i.e. 'velocity') or 'Δv' ["delta v"][2] i.e. the change in velocity – the force which is actually transmitted to/experienced by the Claimant's vehicle and thus the Claimant, by reason of the impact.

In order to make good the assertion that a collision was incapable of causing injury Defendant's often rely on a variety of evidence from varying sources, including: (i) an account from the Defendant driver him/herself as to the movement of his/her vehicle immediately before, and at the time of, impact; the speeds involved; how he/she experienced the collision etc.; (ii) photographic evidence of damage to the vehicle and/or their positioning post-accident; (iii) expert engineering evidence; and (iv) medico-legal evidence. The ultimate goal for any Defendant is, essentially, to present to the Court a persuasive account of an insignificant, mere touching of the two vehicles.

Although long-standing and reasonably common place, defences asserting LVI are not without their controversy or difficulties. It is beyond the scope of this publication to consider the specific medical and technical engineering detail relating to LVI cases. What can be said,

---

[2]   i.e. the change/difference in 'v' – velocity

however, is that whilst general understanding of this particular field (sometimes referred to as 'biomechanics') has greatly improved, there are still wide divergences of respectable opinion in relation to critical issues that arise in such claims. By way of illustrative example: there continues to be serious disagreement between experts as to whether there is, in fact, any 'v' figure below which it can be reliably concluded that injury becomes unlikely/highly unlikely/impossible; with some arguing that no such figure even exists. Whilst it may be possible to ascertain, scientifically, the level of *force* transmitted from one vehicle to another (by assuming various speeds, point of impact, specific vehicle bumper specifications etc.) some point to a long list of other variable factors which, it is argued, have a bearing on whether injury is, or is not, likely to be suffered by an occupant of the vehicle. These include:

- A Claimant's age;

- A Claimant's gender;

- A Claimant's previous medical history (both generally and in relation to spinal conditions specifically);

- A Claimant's general vulnerability to injury;

- A Claimant's previous accident history;

- Whether a Claimant was aware of the impending collision and/or whether he/she was braced at the point of impact, or not;

- The precise position of a Claimant's head/neck at the point of collision;

- The presence/absence of head restraint;

- The age of the Claimant's vehicle;

- The design and construction of the Claimant's vehicle's bumpers;

- The angle and precise position of impact from the Defendant's vehicle.

Given there is no consensus on whether there is actually a 'v' figure below which it can reliably be concluded injury is unlikely, it is wholly unsurprising that there also continues to be disagreement on what any such 'v' figure actually is. With such crucially important matters still being the subject of ongoing academic and expert debate, it is easy to see why LVI cases are not entirely straightforward.

Furthermore, LVI issues routinely arise in low value personal injury claims which, on their face, would objectively warrant allocation to the Fast Track given the value of injuries alleged. However, a Defendant's desire for expert evidence to support an allegation of LVI has ultimately led to LVI defences causing a number of case management difficulties *vis-à-vis* appropriate track and permission for expert evidence, which has required the Court of Appeal's consideration on more than one occasion. This publication considers the two key Court of Appeal decisions later, in Chapter 4, and the way in which LVI defences should be approached procedurally.

CHAPTER TWO

HALLMARKS OF A
LVI COLLISION

In light of the previous Chapter's introductory overview, it is logical to turn in the first instance to consider what hallmarks should be borne in mind when considering whether a claim is likely to be a LVI case, or not. An appreciation of, and ability to identify, the signs or hallmarks indicative of a LVI case are crucial for both Claimant solicitors and Defendant insurers:

- For Claimant solicitors, being able to identify such signs provides an opportunity to promptly investigate such matters with the Claimant(s) and take relevant instructions, as well as to bring to the Claimant's attention the potential that such arguments may be raised by the Defendant, and the risks inherent in pursuing such a claim unsuccessfully; it enables further documentation/evidence to be collated early in the litigation process to 'shore up' any perceived weaknesses in the claim, thereby ensuring that such evidence is not lost or later becomes unavailable; it affords an early opportunity to obtain further supportive expert evidence (most obviously engineering evidence) which can be deployed; it provides an opportunity for a stronger, more persuasive case to be presented in the first instance, thereby possibly satisfying/neutralising any concerns the Defendant's insurer may have been harbouring, thereby prompting them to abandon any intention to raise LVI as an issue; and, in the event that LVI is ultimately raised, whether in the Defence or beforehand, it enables a strong, swift response to be provided. Ultimately, spotting the signs of a potential LVI claim in early course, and seeking to address them, is likely to place the Claimant on the front foot in the litigation;

- For Defendant insurers, being able to identify such signs means that a full and thorough investigation into the circumstances of the collision can be undertaken; it emphasises the need to make early contact with the insured driver in order to secure their co-operation in the defence of the litigation, and so that a contemporaneous version of events can be taken from them; it will enable the identification of any other relevant witnesses of fact; it will ensure the collation and preservation of any relevant documentary evidence; it will guarantee that the LVI issue is raised in the appropriate manner, and at the appropriate time, in accordance with the Court of Appeal's guidance; and, fundamentally, it will facilitate the detection and appropriate defence of potentially dishonest claims.

Each case will naturally turn on its own facts and there will be some (perhaps many) instances where a particular characteristic(s) of the collision or its surrounding circumstances put a Claimant and/or Defendant on notice of a potential LVI defence. However, experience suggests that the following list represents a number of the more commonplace hallmarks to look for:

1. **The accounts provided by the drivers/occupants of the vehicles**

   Naturally, the drivers and any other occupants of the relevant vehicles should be spoken to and their version of events recorded.

   For a LVI defence to be meaningfully pursued by a Defendant, the collision must objectively *look* and *appear* to be towards the more minor end of any imaginable 'seriousness/significance' spectrum of RTAs. It would be wholly unrealistic for a Defendant to mount a defence of LVI where, for example, the photographic evidence very obviously demonstrated a collision of some magnitude (for example: the Claimant's bumper caved in and boot crumpled, the Claimant's rear windscreen shattered, and the Defendant's bonnet concertinaed to half its normal size).

However, there will likely be a difference of account between the Claimant(s) and Defendant driver as to the *perceived* seriousness/force of the collision. How great that disparity in reporting/description is will vary from case to case. It should be borne in mind that the occupants of the two vehicles are likely to experience the accident differently – often a Claimant is unaware of an impending impact and therefore has no time to prepare themselves or brace for the contact, arguably leading to an increase/exacerbation in their subjective experiencing of the collision. Moreover, people inherently describe experiencing the same events differently – if you were to independently ask four people who were present in a vehicle to rate the severity of a collision on a scale from 0 – 10 after it had happened, you might reasonably get four different numbered responses.

It is likely that a Claimant (and any other occupant of the Claimant's vehicle – whether themselves bringing a claim, or not) will describe a collision which is more than merely trifling, but the *actual* description could conceivably range from (i) something which is not realistically too much more significant than 'more than merely trifling'; to (ii) something which is appreciably and objectively significantly more serious. It is, however, not uncommon to see a description by the Claimant(s) which objectively appears minor but which, nonetheless, they assert was sufficient to cause injury. Ultimately, *whatever* description is given by the Claimant(s), they will be alleging that the collision was sufficient to cause the injuries complained of.

The Claimants' account should be carefully scrutinised by both his/her own lawyers, and by the Defendant's advisors: (i) where the Claimant describes a very minor impact, this may tend to suggest that injury was unlikely to have been suffered; any such account should be critically compared with the other objective evidence available to ascertain whether it is supportive of the assertion of injury, or not; (ii) similarly, if a Claimant provides a description which is out of all meaningful comparison/

proportion to the objective evidence obtained then serious contemplation should be given to whether the Claimant's account is plausible in the circumstances (for example, if they describe the collision as being a 10/10 severity which caused their vehicle to be shunted forward 15 metres in the collision but the photographs show very little, if any, damage to the rear of the Claimant's vehicle, and no damage to the front of the Defendant's vehicle). In most cases, it is suggested that a Claimant's version of events is likely to fall somewhere (in the very wide expanse) between the two extremes posited in this paragraph.

As regards the Defendant, it must be recognised that not every LVI defence benefits from the co-operation of the Defendant driver him/herself; sometimes the defence is mounted by the insurer based on other evidence, absent their insured driver's account.

However, where the Defendant driver is involved in the litigation process, one would assume that he/she will have described the collision as being very minor in its nature; this must logically be the case because a contrary account from the Defendant driver, which indicates a more significant/substantial impact/collision, is one which ought to lead any reasonable Defendant litigator to the conclusion that a LVI defence is unsustainable. If the Defendant describes the collision in terms that indicate it was a more than minor contact, serious thought should be given as to whether a LVI defence is reasonably arguable, at all. As already mentioned above, different individuals experience the same collision differently. However, individuals also have pre-conceived ideas as to how serious a collision needs to be before it is likely to cause another person injury; very often these assumptions are illuminating (and, unfortunately for Defendant's, often wrong). It is normally useful to ask the Defendant driver in conference how fast he/she believes a car needs to be travelling at the point of collision in order for it to cause injury to an occupant of the vehicle struck; the answers are sometimes surprising. It is not unusual for drivers to express the view that they need to be travelling at 10mph, 15mph or even more before it is possible that an occupant of the vehicle they hit could suffer injury. Such a belief is wrong; injury can and does occur at much lower speeds. However, it is highly informative as to how quickly the Defendant was probably travelling at the point of impact if they hold such views, and also how significant the collision actually was as a matter of fact.

On both sides of these cases, the benefit of an early, full conference with the client (preferably with Counsel) cannot be overstated. It allows for a proper investigation into the account which the witness is likely to give in due course and significantly informs whether allegations of LVI should be raised and/or sustained by the Defendant and whether any such allegations are likely to be overcome by the Claimant.

Whilst it would be unwise to suggest a template to be applied to every conference in a potential LVI case, consideration of the following matters may be thought relevant:

(a) The witness's subjective assessment of the quality of their recollection of events – a witness who themselves believes their account to be hazy or poor is unlikely to be a persuasive witness in due course;

(b) The weather and road conditions at the time – this may assist in informing potential visibility and stopping distances at the time of the collision;

(c) The degree and nature of traffic at the time – this may assist in determining whether the Defendant's vehicle was/was not likely to have been able to travel at any great speed prior to impact;

(d) Whether the witness was aware of the other vehicle's presence pre-accident – this may assist in informing whether they were conscious of the vehicle and can therefore accurately describe what actually happened at the point of collision and, in relation to the Defendant specifically, whether they were cognisant of the presence of the vehicle which they ultimately contacted;

(e) Whether the Claimant and Defendant's vehicles were, at any stage, stationary prior to collision and, if so, how far away from one another they were – this may inform whether the Defendant was likely to have been able to accelerate to/achieve/maintain any significant speed over the distance between the two vehicles. If, for example, the two cars were in stationary traffic with the Defendant only one metre behind the Claimant's vehicle and the Claimant remained stationary throughout, it would be unlikely that the Defendant could achieve, say, 20mph, by the point of collision;

(f) How fast each witness alleges their vehicle was travelling, and the other vehicle was travelling, as at the point of collision; as well as the basis on which they assert they can be confident of those speeds;

(g) What, if anything, the witness heard at the point of collision – objectively a loud noise e.g. a bang, may indicate a more significant impact. Hearing nothing at all would suggest a minor impact;

(h) Whether the witness felt the collision at all, and if so, how they describe that feeling – the absence of any feeling of collision and/or appreciation that the vehicles had actually touched may indicate a low impact collision; conversely, feeling the impact whether as jolt or similar, may indicate a more forceful connection;

(i) Whether the witness in fact *knew* at the time that there had been a collision, or whether they were unsure/did not believe there had actually been a collision – it is not uncommon for Defendants to indicate they were not actually sure that the vehicles had even touched, which it might be suggested is indicative of a light/negligible impact;

(j) The respective positioning of both vehicles at the point of impact i.e. was this a direct rear end shunt, or was it, say, a glancing blow as the Defendant tried to move passed the Claimant's vehicle? – this may well indicate the level of force likely to be transmitted and the likelihood of occupant displacement;

(k) Whether anything was moved/dislodged in the vehicle at the precise point of impact – for example, if the Claimant had a backpack on the passenger seat which was dislodged onto the floor as a result of the collision, that may indicate that a more significant force was involved;

(l) Whether the occupant was moved in their seat on contact and if so, how – the absence of any movement not only suggests that the collision was of minimal force, but also likely negates (or at least diminishes) the possibility that injury could have been sustained due to the lack of occupant displacement;

(m) Whether the witness's seat belt locked on impact – the activation of the seatbelt restraining mechanism is likely indicative of a more significant force being involved;

(n) Whether the Claimant's vehicle was shunted in the collision – a shunt is indicative of a greater impact force being applied by the Defendant's vehicle;

(o) A description of the damage observed (if any) to both vehicles;

(p) Whether the Claimant complained of injury at the scene and/or appeared to be injured;

(q) Whether the Defendant was him/herself injured – whilst it does not follow axiomatically that where the Defendant is injured, the Claimant would also suffer injury in the same collision, it is almost certainly fatal to a LVI defence if the Defendant confirms they were injured.

2. **The locus and prevailing road layout**

In conjunction with taking full instructions from the witness it is also useful to consider the accident locus, road layout and positioning of street furniture in order to assess whether the alleged mechanism and speed of the collision is, in fact, objectively consistent and/or plausible, in light of the prevailing topography. It is now very easy to visualise discrete loci through Google Maps Street View and, with the help of the historic imaging function[3], it is possible to view the incident location at various dates. It may well be the case after reviewing a particular locus that the alleged circumstances of the accident do not make logical sense and/or appear unlikely. Early acquisition of such knowledge is instructive and can inform whether a LVI defence is sustainable.

3. **Photographs of any damage to the vehicles**

It is crucially important to obtain, as soon as possible, any and all photographs taken by the witnesses. These must be acquired early in the litigation process in order to (i) ensure that a full

---

3   Appearing in a drop-down menu at the top left of an individual Street View

assessment of the merits of a LVI defence can be ascertained; and (ii) to ensure that the photographs are preserved for later use; far too often photographs are deleted, lost, or become inaccessible when they are requested later in the litigation process.

Ideally, full, high quality, colour images should be obtained. In the modern world, the capabilities of many smart phones should make this objective reasonably easy to fulfil.

When considering the utility of the photographs, they are likely to fall into two main categories:

(a) Photographs of the damage to one, other, or both vehicles

These photographs are, perhaps, the most important. They enable an objective appraisal of the damage sustained (if any) to either vehicle. The absence of any obvious visible damage may be just as probative as the appearance of damage. At trial, the Judge will be entitled to consider what the photographs tend to suggest in relation to the severity of the collision, so it is important that an honest assessment of the photographs is undertaken early on.

The photographs must be considered in their totality, but it may be useful, for example, to consider matters such as:

- Do the photographs demonstrate obvious panel distortion or displacement or do the panels appear in their 'normal' place and unmoved?

- Does the damage have the appearance of denting, cracking, splitting or perhaps piercing (sometimes seen in a rear end shunt when, by reason of the force of the impact, the Claimant's bumper is deformed in a concave manner and in the process is pierced by a part of the vehicle hidden behind the bumper itself, before reforming back into its usual shape), or is the damage more akin to scuff marks or scratching or limited only to the paintwork?

- Is the damage widespread, or is it localised to one particular area? If localised, how large is that area of damage?

- Has there been any paint transfer from one vehicle to the other?

- In a typical rear end shunt, was the collision sufficient to crack/break either number plate?

- Where photographs are available of both vehicles, is the damage seen on one/both, consistent with the appearance of the other vehicle? For example, in a 'square on' rear end shunt, damage to the Claimant's nearside rear door would not be what one would expect to see in any photographs produced.

(b) Photographs of the positioning of the vehicles and the road layout

These photographs also play a useful role in assessing the likely severity and magnitude of the vehicles as they will show the positioning of each vehicle post impact. Of course, prior to such photographs being taken one, or other, or both vehicles *may* have been moved; photographs after the vehicles have been moved are less helpful. However, in some instances witnesses exit their respective vehicles immediately following the collision, without either vehicle having been moved – in those cases any photographs demonstrating whether the two vehicles are still touching one another, or not, are important: (i) if they remain touching, that may well be indicative of a minor impact having taken place; (ii) if they are not touching and there is a gap between them, that may well suggest that the Claimant's vehicle was shunted/pushed as a result of the collision, indicative of a more significant impact.

These photographs may also show other useful information, for example:

(a) The presence of any skid marks – indicative of a greater pre-accident speed;

(b) The presence and location of any fallen debris from either vehicle – if, for example, the Claimant's rear nearside light cluster was broken in the collision, it may be visible on the road surface and may indicate the point of collision itself.

4. **Any other objective evidence of the likely magnitude of the impact**

In some instances, there may be additional, objective evidence available, which assists in the assessment of the likely magnitude of, and circumstances surrounding, the impact. Some more common examples include:

(a) Dashcam footage – a number of recent national surveys have suggested that somewhere between 25 – 50% of motorists now use a dashcam in their vehicle. It will not have escaped any road user that there has been a significant increase in use of such cameras over recent years. Mostly, dashcam footage is taken from the front of the vehicle i.e. looking through the front windscreen, although in some instances dashcam footage is also available from a rearward looking perspective. Some dashcams are more advanced than others (for example, some include audio recording as well) but, fundamentally, *any* dashcam footage will be instructive, perhaps highly so, as it will show the collision actually take place.

As regards any *forward* facing dashcam footage it is often possible to discern the following important matters:

i. The prevailing traffic conditions on approach to the accident locus;

ii. An *impression* of how fast the vehicle was moving (if at all) prior to impact;

iii. Whether either vehicle was stationary at any stage immediately prior to impact;

iv. When, if at all, the Defendant driver braked prior to impact, as well as the nature of the braking – was it early and progressive, or was it late and sharp?;

v. Any noise made in the either vehicle on impact;

vi. Whether the Claimant's vehicle is visibly moved or shunted on impact.

As regards any *rearward* facing dashcam footage, it is likely that such evidence will come from the Claimant's vehicle and may well show:

i. The Defendant's speed on approach;

ii. Whether, and if so when, the Defendant appeared to slow in advance of the collision;

iii. The Defendant driver's reaction in his/her own car, immediately prior to and post impact;

    iv.   Whether the Claimant's vehicle is visibly moved or shunted on impact.

(b) Tachographs (or similar) – in some commercial vehicles the moving time(s) and speeds of the vehicle are continuously recorded. Such information should be obtained in order to investigate the *actual* speed of the vehicle immediately prior to, and at the point of, impact. Such data should also confirm the nature and extent of any braking applied.

(c) CCTV footage – it may be such footage is available, for example, from nearby shops/business premises. If it can be obtained, it may assist in visualising the collision take place.

5.   **The engineering evidence relied on by the Claimant**

In most cases, together with the claim for injury, a Claimant is likely to present a claim for property damage to the vehicle itself (whether by way of repairs or for the pre-accident value following a conclusion that the vehicle is a total loss); should no claim for vehicle repairs be advanced this should be investigated – has the Claimant simply elected not to bother pursuing such a claim, or is the absence of such a claim because there was, in fact, no discernible damage to the vehicle at all?

Where a claim for property damage is brought, the Claimant is overwhelmingly likely to rely on a report from a motor engineer/assessor, setting out the nature and extent of the damage sustained, together with costings for repair. Those acting in this field of the law will be more than familiar with such reports.

It is not possible to say that a repair costing above/below "£x" is one which the Court is likely to consider is/is not a low-velocity impact; each case will turn on its own facts. Naturally, some vehicles are inherently just more expensive to repair than others; generally, the more prestigious a vehicle, the more money it will costs to repair it [rear bumper damage caused to an Aston Martin DB9 will cost more to repair than identical damage caused to the rear of a Ford Focus]. This difference in the inherent cost of repair as between different types of vehicles is something that has to be kept in mind.

Accordingly, the *content* of the relevant report(s) must be considered carefully. In particular, close attention should be paid not just to the *overall* anticipated cost of repairs (not least because of the inherent difference in anticipated cost of repairs given the prestigiousness of the vehicle), but to the specific constituent elements of the overall cost. In an ordinary case, the overall figure will likely comprise the costs of:

(a) Labour;

(b) Paint/Materials;

(c) Parts; and

(d) Extras.

Of these the most important are often (b) Paint/Materials; and (c) Parts, as they enable an assessment of what was *actually* damaged on the vehicle and therefore what actually needed to be repaired/replaced. Labour charges may fluctuate significantly (both in relation to number of hours spent and hourly rate applied) – simply looking at how *long* a repair is anticipated to take, or how *much* the labour cost will be, may give a misleading impression as to the overall severity of the damage sustained. In the example given above, one would *expect* the labour costs for a repair to an Aston Martin DB9 to be appreciable: it is a prestige vehicle, likely requiring specialist mechanics to undertake the repair, who are therefore likely to be able to charge more per hour for their work. However, a careful review of the paint/materials and parts required indicates what physical insult was caused to the Claimant's vehicle.

Therefore, in circumstances where the repair costs overall appear not insignificant, where, say, 90% of those costs relate to labour and extras, it may well still be a case in which a LVI defence can be sustainably advanced. Conversely, where a close analysis of the Claimant's report indicates that there was a significant amount of damage caused to the vehicle which required extensive new parts or re-painting, it may well indicate that a LVI defence has little to no prospects of success.

6. **Any engineering evidence in relation to the Defendant's vehicle**

Depending on when the Claimant first intimates their claim it may be that the Defendant has already arranged to have their vehicle inspected/assessed (such information will only be available, initially at least, to the Defendant's advisors). The information contained within that report will enable the Defendant to consider whether the damage to his/her own vehicle is indicative of a low-velocity impact, or not. The same considerations as set out in the immediately preceding sub-paragraph apply with equal force to the Defendant's own assessor's report.

7. **The medico-legal evidence served with the Particulars of Claim**

A Claimant will, in the ordinary run of things, support their case with at least one medical report served with the proceedings (of course, further reports may follow in due course, if required). It is important to consider the content of the initial medical report(s), not least to review the manner in which the collision is described by the Claimant to the doctor; the severity of collision alleged; and whether they were moved (and if so how) on impact. These are matters which, although not determinative at an early stage of the litigation, go into the balance when considering whether a LVI defence is likely to arise or can be sensibly pursued. They are also matters which take on further relevance at trial, once the evidence has crystallised, in so far as they may be consistent or inconsistent with the Claimant's other reporting to other medico-legal experts and in their witness statement.

CHAPTER THREE

PRE-ACTION CONDUCT

The Protocol for Low Value Personal Injury Claims in Road Traffic Accidents

The majority of claims involving LVI allegations will fall within the scope of The Protocol for Low Value Personal Injury Claims in Road Traffic Accidents ("PAP"), in force from 31st July 2013 onwards (as amended)[4]. As at the date of publication of this work, the Scope of the PAP is confirmed in paragraph 4.1:

4.1 This Protocol applies where—

(1) a claim for damages arises from a road traffic accident occurs on or after 31st May 2021[5];

(2) the claim includes damages in respect of personal injury;

(3) the claimant values the claim at no more than the Protocol upper limit; and

---

[4]   Most notably in relation to claims arising in relation to accidents which take place on or after 31st May 2021 to take account of the effects of the Whiplash Injury Regulations 2021 (SI 2021/642).

[5]   In relation to accidents taking place before 31st May 2021, the earlier version of the PAP provided a date of 31st July 2013 in paragraph 4.1(1) but the remainder of paragraph 4.1 was otherwise identical. Paragraph 4.2(1) confirms that the earlier version of the PAP as it stood immediately before 31st May 2021 continues to apply to all accidents taking place before 31st May 2021 [save in relation to those which occurred before 31st July 2013, to which the original version of the PAP will apply – although such cases will likely be rare given their historic nature].

(4) if proceedings were started the small claims track would not be the normal track for that claim.

There are various exceptions to the applicability of the PAP (for example in relation to children and vulnerable road users)[6] , the consideration of which falls outside the scope of this work.

In the ordinary way, in accordance with paragraph 6.1 et seq., a Claimant must complete and send a Claims Notification Form ("CNF") to the Defendant's insurer; the Defendant's insurer must acknowledge receipt of the CNF in accordance with paragraph 6.10 and respond substantively within 15 days in accordance with paragraph 6.11.

In accordance with paragraph 6.15, a claim will no longer continue under the PAP where (emphasis added):

Contributory negligence, liability not admitted or failure to respond

> **6.15** The claim will no longer continue under this Protocol where the defendant, within the period in paragraph 6.11 or 6.13—
>
> (1) makes an admission of liability but alleges contributory negligence (other than in relation to the claimant's admitted failure to wear a seat belt);
>
> (2) does not complete and send the CNF response;
>
> **(3) does not admit liability; or**
>
> (4) notifies the claimant that the defendant considers that—
>
> > (a) there is inadequate mandatory information in the CNF; or

---

[6] See for example: PAP paragraphs 4.1 and 4.1A and CPR r. 26.6A and B; and PAP paragraph 4.5.

(b) if proceedings were issued, the small claims track would be the normal track for that claim.

Accordingly, where the Defendant's insurer does not "admit liability", the claim will 'fall out' of the Protocol process.

An admission of liability is defined in paragraph 1.1(1) as (emphasis added):

(1) 'admission of liability' means the defendant admits that—

(a) the accident occurred;

(b) the accident was caused by the defendant's breach of duty;

(c) the defendant caused some loss to the claimant, the nature and extent of which is not admitted; and

(d) the defendant has no accrued defence to the claim under the Limitation Act 1980;

As noted in Chapter 1, a LVI defence is a challenge to the causation of injury. In such circumstances, the Defendant's insurer could not make an 'admission of liability' as defined because the Defendant's position is that the collision was incapable of causing any injury, and the claim will therefore drop from the Protocol process.

The effect of dropping from the Protocol process is described in paragraph 6.17:

6.17 Where paragraph 6.15 applies the claim will proceed under the Pre-Action Protocol for Personal Injury Claims starting at paragraph 6.3 of that Protocol (which allows a maximum of three months for the defendant to investigate the claim) except that where paragraph 6.15(4)(a) applies the claim will proceed under paragraph 5.1 of that Protocol.

Thus, having exited the Portal process, the claim will then continue under the Pre-Action Protocol for Personal Injury Claims ("PI PAP"), commencing at paragraph 6.3. In most circumstances[7] the CNF can be used as the letter of claim for the purpose of the PI PAP[8].

It is worth noting the provisions of paragraph 6.16 of the PAP:

> **6.16** Where the defendant does not admit liability under paragraph 6.15(3), the defendant must give brief reasons in the CNF response.

It is suggested that in accordance with paragraph 6.16, the Defendant's insurer's response to the CNF should, where possible, make clear that it considers the case to be a low-velocity impact.

Pre-Action Protocol for Personal Injury Claims

Of note, paragraph 6.3 of the PI PAP provides a maximum of three months from the date of acknowledgment of the Letter of Claim (or, more realistically, the CNF) to investigate. By the end of that three-month period the Defendant insurer should reply stating if liability is admitted which, for the purpose of paragraph 6.3, includes an admission that "...*the claimant suffered loss...*". In a LVI situation this is not an admission that a Defendant insurer could make.

Paragraph 6.1 of the PI PAP refers to a proposed template for the Defendant's Letter of Response. It is interesting to note that within that template, under the heading "Liability" is suggested, as one possible response:

> "*In respect of our client's liability for this accident we*

---

[7]   Save where the CNF contained inadequate information

[8]   See: PI PAP paragraph 5.5.1.

[...]

admit the accident occurred but deny that our client is responsible for any loss or damage alleged to have been caused for the following reasons:- "

It appears, therefore, that the pro forma template response envisages the Defendant's insurer providing reasons as to why, although it is accepted that an accident took place, the *damage* i.e. personal injury, alleged was not caused by the Defendant. It seems clear that any Defendant insurer seeking to raise the issue of LVI should do so within the initial Letter of Response in order to comply with the requirements of the PI PAP.

In addition, the position is confirmed by paragraph 6.5 (emphasis added):

6.5 If a defendant denies liability **and/or causation, their version of events should be supplied.** The **defendant should also enclose with the response, documents in their possession which are material to the issues between the parties,** and which would be likely to be ordered to be disclosed by the court, either on an application for pre-action disclosure, or on disclosure during proceedings. No charge will be made for providing copy documents under the Protocol.

Paragraph 6.5 is important. The conduct expected of the Defendant includes:

- That the Defendant gives a version of events. It is suggested that this requires not just a bald statement that the Defendant considers it to be a low-velocity impact (that would arguably not be a "version of events" at all, but simply confirmation of the Defendant's position) but rather an account as to *why* and on *what grounds* the Defendant considers that the collision was insufficient to cause injury to the Claimant(s); and

- Disclosure of relevant documentation in the Defendant's possession. Logically this would include: any photographs; dashcam footage; and any engineering evidence concerning the Defendant's vehicle (if such exists). The PI PAP supports early exchange of relevant documentation, in an attempt to avoid litigated proceedings being issued.

Furthermore, at paragraph 7.1 the PI PAP provides as follows in relation to disclosure:

7.1 Documents

7.1.1 The aim of early disclosure of documents by the defendant is not to encourage 'fishing expeditions' by the claimant, but to promote an early exchange of relevant information to help in clarifying or resolving issues in dispute. The claimant's solicitor can assist by identifying in the Letter of Claim or in a subsequent letter the particular categories of documents which they consider are relevant and why, with a brief explanation of their purported relevance if necessary.

7.1.2 Attached at Annexe C are specimen, but non-exhaustive, lists of documents likely to be material in different types of claim.

7.1.3 Pre-action disclosure will generally be limited to the documents required to be enclosed with the Letter of Claim and the Response. In cases where liability is admitted in full, disclosure will be limited to the documents relevant to quantum, the parties can agree that further disclosure may be given. If either or both of the parties consider that further disclosure should be given but there is disagreement about some aspect of that process, they may be able to make an application to the court for pre-action disclosure under Part 31 of the CPR. Parties should assist each other and avoid the necessity for such an application.

7.1.4 The protocol should also contain a requirement that the defendant is under a duty to preserve the disclosure documents and other evidence (CCTV for example). If the documents are destroyed, this could be an abuse of the court process.

Reference to Annexe C is instructive. Section A of Annexe C provides:

SECTION A

In all cases where liability is at issue–

(i) documents identifying nature, extent and location of damage to defendant's vehicle where there is any dispute about point of impact;

[…]

In a LVI case liability would be "in issue". Whilst Section A(i) is, strictly, limited to a dispute about the *"point of impact"* it is arguable that this includes any photographs and engineering evidence that the Defendant may have in their possession where there is a challenge to the nature and extent of damage to either vehicle. Certainly, in this regard, it is suggested that the spirit of the PI PAP (if not the precise letter of Section A(i)) would support a need for disclosure of such documentation in early course.

Failures of Pre-Action Conduct

If either Claimant or Defendant considers that there has been a failure to comply with the pre-action obligations imposed by both applicable Pre-Action Protocols and, in particular, a failure to give voluntary disclosure of relevant documentation, then consideration should be given to issuing an application for pre-action disclosure in accordance with CPR r. 31.16. It is likely that such applications will be of most benefit to Claimant solicitors in circumstances where, having set out the Claimant's case and provided relevant document in anticipation of prompt settlement of the claim, they may become aware of documents held by the Defendant which are not forthcoming but which, objectively, need to be reviewed. It may be of most benefit to Defendants in relation to medical records, particularly where the medical evidence demonstrates that the Claimant's own expert(s) has already reviewed the notes in the preparation of his/her report, or photographic evidence if it is clear that some photographs were taken by the Claimant's engineer but have not been provided with his/her report.

Such applications are likely to meet the jurisdictional threshold set out in r. 31.16(3). The Court retains a discretion to order such disclosure but so ordering is quite likely to facilitate a saving in both time and costs, by ensuring appropriate documentation is provided in early course thereby enabling the party making the application to take an objective view on the prospects of success of any LVI defence. It may ultimately lead to the Claimant abandoning what transpires to be a hopeless claim; or the Defendant abandoning a weak LVI defence and thereafter settling the claim.

CHAPTER FOUR

THE TWO KEY COURT
OF APPEAL CASES:
KEARSLEY AND *CASEY*

On two key occasions the Court of Appeal has been asked to consider issues surrounding low-velocity impact cases, notably how such cases should be case managed and what steps should be taken, by the parties and the Court, in order to prepare such matters efficiently, and proportionately, for trial. Anyone practising in this area of the law must ensure they are fully familiar with the authoritative guidance given by the Court of Appeal in both cases, and a careful reading of both judgments is essential.

Alan Mark Kearsley v Daniel Klarfeld [2005] EWCA Civ 1510

Background

The Claimant was involved in a RTA on 22nd July 2003. Breach of duty was admitted but causation was in issue, with the Defendant's insurer having paid for the costs of repairs to the Claimant's car. The Defendant's account of the incident was that he had stopped a few feet behind the Claimant's car and that whilst he was waiting for the Claimant to move forward his foot slipped off the clutch and his car collided with the rear of the vehicle in front [a commonplace LVI scenario].

The Claimant brough a claim for personal injury supported by a medical report from a Dr Picardo (GP) who concluded that the Claimant had suffered a soft tissue injury to his neck and upper back from which he would recover within about eight months; it was described as a 'mild to moderate whiplash injury'.

The Defendant obtained a report from a Mr Ralph of Northern Assessors [a motor vehicle assessor company]. On the basis of the instructions he received, Mr Ralph concluded that the collision had taken place when the Defendant was moving at less than 3mph and that in such circumstances, the collision would not have caused any unusual force to be applied to the Claimant as he sat in his car.

The Defendant put Part 35 questions to Dr Picardo on the assumption that the Defendant's car was travelling at low velocity.

The claim was then issued.

The Defendant provided an amended Defence in which it referred to Mr Ralph's report and the evidence of a Mr Newman (a Consultant Orthopaedic Surgeon and Traumatologist) who had prepared a report without having examined the Claimant, and asserted that on the basis of those reports that the Defendant's case was that the Claimant was fabricating his symptoms and he had sustained no injuries in the collision.

The claim was allocated to the Fast Track (both parties having requested such allocation in their respective Directions Questionnaires) and the court gave permission for the Claimant to rely on Dr Picardo's report, and for the Defendant to rely on Mr Newman and Mr Ralph's reports.

Shortly after the Order was sealed, the Defendant filed further documents with the Court and requested that the claim be allocated to the Multi Track, together with permission for the experts to give oral evidence at trial, in part on the basis that the Defendant was making serious allegations and those allegations could only be properly dealt with by the parties calling expert evidence as they saw fit. The Court took no action in response to the Defendant's request.

Dr Picardo provided a further letter in which he reiterated his belief that the Claimant was suffering with a mild whiplash injury and provided some medical literature tending to suggest that there was no strong correlation between the extent of vehicle damage and the injuries sustained in minor collisions.

A short while later, the Claimant's solicitors evinced an intention to call evidence from a more specialist medical expert. They subsequently disclosed a report from a Mr Nee, an Orthopaedic Surgeon, who professed to have a special interest in injuries allegedly sustained in low velocity collisions. Mr Nee had examined the Claimant and credited his symptoms; he also expressed doubt about the validity of Mr Ralph's conclusions.

The Defendant's solicitor indicated to the Claimant's solicitors that oral evidence from the experts was necessary and two days were required for trial and that the matter should be re-allocated. The Claimant applied for reallocation to the Multi Track and permission to call Mr Nee instead of Dr Picardo. The Defendant opposed the application in so far as it related to the Claimant having permission to call evidence from Mr Nee.

First Instance Decision

The District Judge considered that nothing material had changed since the directions were given; she was concerned that the directions now being sought were disproportionate – this was a relatively low value claim and she had to bear in mind the proportionality of the costs and expense. She considered that the way the evidence of Mr Newman was put was going to come down to the credibility of the Claimant at trial. She could not see that it was a case which ought to be completely re-tracked and re-timetabled, with the trial window being extended and the trial being extended to two days. She directed a joint meeting between Mr Newman and Dr Picardo and refused to permit any oral evidence (at [15]).

First Appeal

The Claimant was granted permission to appeal that decision.

On a first appeal, HHJ Tetlow highlighted the need to have regard to the Overriding Objective and that 'justice should be done'; he noted that the Claimant was a 45 year-old male nurse and if fraud were found against him there might be more serious consequences than just losing the case. The Judge considered that an allegation of fraud was one which needed to be taken seriously, with a proper examination of the issues at trial. HHJ Tetlow considered that the District Judge was wrong not to have revisited the Court's initial directions order, and that she should have concluded that, because this was a fraud case, it should in the Multi Track. Further, the District Judge should have realised that unless Dr Picardo and Mr Newman were going to suddenly agree, they should have been called to give oral evidence; as would Mr Ralph. The Judge observed that any trial judge faced with the case would have acceded to a request for an adjournment "at vast expense" so that proper expertise could be put in place, and so that an engineer could balance Mr Ralph's evidence, if required.

HHJ Tetlow was firmly of the view that the case should be in the Multi Track, with a two-day time estimate. He also felt that there was inequality of arms and an unlevel playing field in relation to Dr Picardo and Mr Newman's evidence and since the Claimant did not think Dr Picardo was the 'right man', the Court should look again and revisit the order. The Judge gave permission to the Claimant to rely on Mr Nee in place of Dr Picardo and gave permission for an engineering report to be served (at [16] – [21]).

The Defendant appealed.

Court of Appeal

The second appeal raised what the Court of Appeal described as "*a point of practice of general importance*" (at [1]).

Ultimately, the Defendant's appeal was dismissed.

The Court described allegations of LVI as being the latest problem in "*the context of personal injury litigation in this country which cause considerable case-handling complexities in the county courts during the period before law and practice have learned how to accommodate them*" and that "*[W]hen they arise, the same point tends to crop up again and again all over the country, usually in connection with comparatively low value litigation*" (at [22]).

The Court referred to two decisions: (i) *Armstrong v First York Ltd* [2005] EWCA Civ 277[9], in which the trial Judge HHJ Stewart QC had been impressed by the evidence of a forensic engineer who gave evidence on behalf of the Defendant and could find no flaw in his evidence, but nevertheless entered judgment for the claimants because of his clear and unequivocal impression of them as witnesses, describing how they gave their evidence in a truthful, honest and guileless way, and spoke of their veracity and straightforwardness; and (ii) *Liprot v Charters* (unreported) in which HHJ Holman had been unimpressed by the Defendant's engineer who gave oral evidence at trial (the same individual who gave evidence on behalf of the Defendant in *Armstrong*); that was particularly so when putting it alongside the expert medical evidence and other evidence the court had received; and found that the claimant was trying to give an honest recollection of events, and that she was not a fraudster advancing a claim which she knew to be false.

---

[9]   Dealt with, in detail, in Chapter 7 below

The Court of Appeal observed that the two cited cases identified the *"contemporary dilemma in stark terms"*. The Court described the dilemma thus (at [28]):

> *"A personal injuries claim which is only just above the small claims limit; an allegation by the defendant's insurers, based on complex theorizing, to the effect that the claimant has set out to present a claim he/she knows to be false; and a reluctance on the part of the defendant's insurers to accept that the court can do justice in relation to liability and causation simply by hearing lay witnesses describe what happened in the accident and by considering written medical evidence about simple injuries, the damage to the vehicles, and the claimant's pre-accident medical state. How is such a case to be fairly tried in less than two days, with time available for the expert evidence to be put to the test by oral evidence and cross-examination?"*

The Court of Appeal held that HHJ Tetlow was right to have overruled the District Judge for the reasons he gave. Due to time pressures at the hearing before her, the District Judge did not adequately address the question of whether the case could be dealt with justly on the Fast Track, or consider whether because fraud was alleged it was necessary in the interests of justice for the experts to attend so that the trial could properly unravel the complexities that were inherent in their contested evidence. Nor had the District Judge considered issues relating to the desirability of equality of arms. Circumstances had changed since the directions were given and both parties had altered their stance and were contending that expert evidence was necessary to deal justly with the Defendant's case, so that a one-day trial in the Fast Track would not achieve justice. The very nature of the issues raised in the Defence required the experts to attend to give oral evidence if justice was to be done.

The Court was informed that different parts of the country were being faced with a vast difference of approach amongst different members of the judiciary and the inconsistency of approach was causing confusion and expense because the same points were being argued in every case with differing results. The Court of Appeal observed at [35]:

"...it appears to us that until some of the issues that arise in these disputes have been authoritatively dissected and analysed at High Court level, it would not be wrong or disproportionate to allocate what would ordinarily be a fast track claim (by reason of its low value) into the multi-track on the grounds that the criteria for the admission of oral expert evidence are satisfied and the trial is therefore likely to last more than one day".

The Court expressed the hope that it may be possible to group a number of cases together before a High Court Judge who could hear a number of experts on each side of the argument and give authoritative guidance on the appropriate approach to some of the generic issues that featured in the instant case. The Court of Appeal also expressed concern that these issues were being litigated on an individual basis at disproportionate expense in quite small claims up and down the country; it further recognised that whilst a High Court judgment in a group of cases would not be able to resolve all the uncertainties, it would likely furnish a more structured framework for judicial decision making than was currently available.

Importantly, the Court of Appeal also gave guidance in relation to two further matters of practice:

First, relating to pleadings, the Court noted that parties should follow the practice of giving full particulars of any allegation of dishonesty or malice and, where any inference of fraud or dishonesty is alleged, the basis on which the inference is alleged should be included. However, the court was puzzled by the practice which had started to emerge in LVI litigation of requiring the defence to include a substantive allegation of fraud or fabrication. Provided a Defendant followed the rules set out in CPR r. 16.5 there was no need for a substantive allegation of fraud or fabrication; it was sufficient to set out fully the facts from which the Defendant would be inviting the Judge to draw the inference that a Claimant had not suffered the injuries he asserted; all that was necessary was to make clear the contentions on which the Defendant would be inviting the Judge to conclude that the Claimant had not proved that which he set out to prove, and therefore dismiss the claim (see: [40] – [49]).

Secondly, the Court sought to offer guidance about how claims such as the instant one could be handled more economically in the future. At [50] the Court stated:

> "*The pre-action protocol should be followed in all cases. We would also endorse the suggestion made by Mr Mark Turner QC that in cases of this kind when intimating a claim the claimant's advisers should offer access to their client's vehicle to the defendant's insurers for the purpose of early examination (if they so wish), and give early disclosure (with irrelevant passages redacted, if necessary) of any contemporaneous GP's or other relevant medical notes. This will enable the defendant's insurers to get hold of relevant evidential material expeditiously and inexpensively, as the nature of these claims requires. In turn, it may be desirable for the defendant's insurers to make it clear that they regard this as a low velocity impact case in which they will be seeking more expensive advice than the value of the claim would justify. We were told that it is customary to wait for up to nine months for such advice, and if they take this step at once (whether or not they ultimately decide to contest the claim along the lines of the amended defence in the present case) both parties will know where they stand at the outset.*"

Comment

On the facts, the ultimate outcome of the appeal in *Kearsley* is not surprising.

Regrettably, the series of test cases envisaged by the Court of Appeal, which were to be tried together by a High Court Judge so that authoritative guidance could be given on some of the generic issues in LVI cases, never materialised. No such guidance was thus ever provided by the High Court.

Kearsley is important, primarily, for the two issues of practice it identified, and in relation to which it sought to give guidance, in paragraphs [40] – [50].

Practice Point 1: Defence Pleadings

The first related to the manner in which a Defendant was required to plead its/his/her case. Pre-*Kearsley* a tendency had arisen for Defendant insurers to file defences positively pleading fraud on the basis of LVI. The Court of Appeal's comments strongly indicate that it is unnecessary for a positive pleading of fraud to be advanced; it is sufficient for a Defendant to simply set out those facts/matters from which the Court will be invited, at trial, to conclude that no injury was sustained. The approach in *Kearsley* was not, at least initially, universally endorsed by the Courts:

Newman v Laver & Anor [2006] EWCA Civ 1135

The correctness of the approach to the pleading of the Defence, as advocated by *Kearsley*, was adopted seemingly without issue in *Newman v Laver & Anor* at [81]:

> *"In my judgment, there was no need of any blanket allegation of fraud, fakery or fabrication in the pleaded defence: see Kearsley v. Klarfeld [2005] EWCA Civ 1510 (unreported, 6 December 2005) , especially at paras 45 and 47/49 (an authority very fairly provided to us by Mr Foskett following the hearing). The defence and its counter schedule of damages, together with the expert reports served pursuant to the defence, and the video provided for trial, sufficiently put in issue the defendant's lack of acceptance that Mr Newman had suffered the injuries and sequelae of which he complained, including in particular BMD (see, for instance para 2 of the counter-schedule). In truth there was no wholesale attack of fabrication, no general attack on Mr Newman's honesty, at trial, as the defendant's written closing submissions demonstrate. Instead, there was, as must occur at the close of many a trial, a detailed submission by reference to specific points*

which had arisen in the evidence as to why the judge should regard Mr Newman's credibility as being both at the heart of his claim and as being suspect. The submission divided its fire between specific allegations of falsehood, exaggeration, and inconsistency, to be balanced, it was said, against the lack of objective verification of the symptoms relied on."

Hussain v Amin [2012] EWCA Civ 1456

However, the correctness of the general approach advocated in *Kearsley* was subsequently called into some doubt by the Court of Appeal in its decision in *Hussain v Amin* in which Davis LJ expressed concern (albeit obiter) about what he described as "hybrid" defences to road traffic accident claims. At [18] – [19] his Lordship said:

"18. I would, however, wish to add my own comments about the pleaded defence of the second defendant [i.e. the relevant insurer]. It was perfectly proper to join issue on the primary facts alleged in the Particulars of Claim and as to whether there had indeed been negligence and whether the claimed losses had been caused thereby. But the pleaded defence went much further in paragraphs 7 and 9, setting out a number of matters which, it was alleged, raised 'significant concerns' as to whether or not this had been a staged accident requiring further investigation. Possibly, although I have my reservations, such a pleading could be justified as an initial holding defence. But it is a case pleaded on insinuation, not allegation. If the second defendant considered that it had sufficient material to justify a plea that the claim was based on a collision which was a sham or a fraud, it behoved it properly and in ample time before trial so to plead in clear and unequivocal terms and with proper particulars. Thereafter the burden of proof would of course have been on the second defendant to establish such a defence.

19. In the event, as I see it, the claimant was faced with a hybrid, he in effect being required at trial to deal with an insinuation of fraud without any express allegation to that effect pleaded. Realistically, the trial judge dealt with the matter in the round, concluding that the claim was not fabricated or fraudulent and that the accident had not been staged. But this sort of pleading should not be sanctioned."

Dyson LJ, then Master of the Rolls, said (at [2]):

"Although the terms of the pleaded defence are not relevant to the issues that have been raised in this appeal, I am bound to register my concern with the way in which what in substance is an allegation of fraud was pleaded."

If, and to the extent that, *Hussain* did cast such doubt on the correctness of the general approach advocated for in *Kearsley*, it is suggested that such doubt has since been quelled, and the correctness of the *Kearsley* approach re-affirmed, as demonstrated in a series of authoritative and persuasive decisions and observations which followed.

Ghulam Safi & Ors v Jowharah Baker & Anor [2013] WL 8467401

In *Ghulam Safi & Ors v Jowharah Baker & Anor*, HHJ Hand QC considered such matters when giving judgment following trial. At trial, the Claimants took issue with the form of the amended Defence and invited the Judge to strike the Defence out (thereby forcing the Defendant to revert to an earlier Defence) on the basis that the amended Defence advanced an insinuation of fraud without an express allegation of fraud. HHJ Hand QC was referred to the passages from *Hussain* quoted above, as well as *Kearsley*, and observed (at [23]):

"There is a distinction, as it seems to me, to be drawn between making an allegation of fraud, on the one hand, and needing necessarily to plead fraud in circumstances where what you are doing is resisting the claim, on the other. To my mind this is what Brooke LJ is pointing out

in these passages[10]. At paragraph 47 of his judgment, the learned Lord Justice of Appeal said, in the context of Rooney v Graves , that His Honour Judge Stewart QC had in that case:

> *"…made a clear distinction between a case in which the defendant makes an allegation of dishonesty based on an expert's report (which in his view entitles the claimant to get his own expert and to have a hearing, whatever the amount involved), and a case where the defendant disavows dishonesty and says that this was no part of his case at all. The judge added:*
>
> > *'I think we have got to make it absolutely clear to the Bar and to judges that 'you are a liar' is something that people are entitled to proper notice of because if that is alleged against them they are entitled, on the face of it, subject to the individual cases, to have expert evidence in support'."*

At [24], HHJ Hand QC observed that,

> *"The argument in this case raises an issue that has been rumbling in this court and in other county courts for some very considerable time. There is nothing unusual about the way in which the amended defence in this case is pleaded. I have seen a number of them myself exactly in this form or in similar form and have no doubt from discussions outside court with my colleagues that they have similarly seen the like and that such defences are a commonplace."*

In considering the substance of the submissions advanced, HHJ Hand QC noted at [25] – [26]:

> *"25. Mr Coulter's argument opens up the question as to the extent to which such defences should be permitted to stand. On the one hand, this defence, as it seems to me, makes quite clear — almost as if it were by way of a series of preformulated questions — what the likely cross-*

---

[10] Paragraphs 48 and 49 of *Kearsley*

examination of the claimants might be. It also makes it quite clear what the engineering evidence in this case might have to contribute. But Mr Coulter's submission is this is not merely courtesy or advance notice, the issue here is where is this all going? Or putting it another way, what closing submission can Mr Hogg make in relation to this material? If the submission that he makes is this is fraud then quite clearly I think everybody would agree that that allegation has to be clearly stated.

26. If, on the other hand, what he wishes to do is to say there are a number of features in this case that should cause the court to examine the claimants' case with great care to decide whether it has been proved on a balance of probabilities, then I think that Brooke LJ would not find that objectionable and would regard that as something that did not need to be pleaded. Indeed, Mr Hogg points out that, before counsel can plead fraud, there must be reasonably credible material that establishes a prima facie case of fraud and evidence put before the court which can make good that allegation. It is a matter of nice judgment as to whether the material available goes beyond that threshold or falls short of it."

In specifically considering the comments of Davis LJ in *Hussain*, HHJ Hand QC observed (at [27] – [28]) (emphasis added):

*27. Intellectually impeccable though the analysis of Davis LJ is in paragraphs 18 and 19 of the judgment in Hussain v Amin and Charters Insurance Limited , **untempered by the way in which an experienced judge at first instance would conduct a trial so as to ensure fairness to the parties, it throws down a gauntlet to the insurers which they will find very difficult to pick up.** And it faces them with the challenge of deciding whether to make the allegation of fraud or, as Davis LJ seems to suggest, simply content themselves with putting the claimant to proof.*

*28. **I am not convinced that Davis LJ intended to bring about a situation in which the defendants could not give notice to the*** *claimants as to what aspects of the case they found odd, inconsistent, discrepant or even unacceptable, on the one hand, but not be able to advance those points because they could be collected together and amount to an insinuation of fraud. I am confident that Davis LJ did not intend to exclude from a case of this sort probing cross-examination that might assist the judge at first instance with issues of credibility and reliability. I do not accept that simply because this type of allegation can lead to what my Lord called an insinuation (and which I might call an inference) is necessarily to exclude it. What the judge at first instance must be alert to is not to make a finding of fraud, in effect, by the back door, without actually making a finding of fraud. The judge must be alert to the danger of putting some sort of burden on the claimant to disprove fraud when fraud has not been alleged, and thus there could be no burden on the claimant."*

It is clear from the language used that HHJ Hand QC's approach was one drawing on the practical experience of first instance trial Judges, and the reality of the situation faced in the County Courts on a day-to-day basis.

Ahmed v Lalik [2015] EWHC 651 (QB)

In *Ahmed v Lalik*, in considering an application for permission to appeal, Cranson J was referred to *Hussain v Amin* and the passages cited immediately above. Cranson J observed (at [24]) (emphasis added):

*"Unfortunately, we do not know the state of the pleadings in Hussain. However, **the concern expressed by Lord Dyson MR and the obiter remarks of Davis LJ in that case should not**, in my view, **be read as casting doubt on well-established authorities such as Kearsley v. Klarfeld [2005] EWCA Civ 1510; [2006] 2 All ER 303, [45], [47]-[49] and Francis v. Wells [2007] EWCA Civ 1350; [2008] RTR 13, [3], which establish that in this type of case (minor road vehicle accidents) it is not necessary for the defence to make a substantive allegation of fraud or fabrication, but it is sufficient to set out the***

detailed facts from which the court would be invited to draw the inference that the claimant has not, in fact, suffered the injuries or damage alleged. These authorities recognise the procedural and ethical inhibitions on advocates alleging fraud and the realities in this type of case for defendant insurance companies unearthing evidence of it."

Aso Yasin v Perhraw Karim, Sabre Insurance [2015] WL 3630428

Two months after the decision was given in *Ahmed v Lalik*, HHJ Jeremy Richardson QC gave judgment in the case of *Aso Yasin v Perhraw Karim, Sabre Insurance*. The case concerned an appeal against the decision of DDJ Godfrey who had struck out several sub-paragraphs of the Defence, which he adjudged to be an allegation of fraud without such an explicit assertion being made. The appeal was allowed. HHJ Richardson QC was referred to both *Hussain v Amin* and *Ahmed v Lalik* and summarised what he considered to be the position at [13] – [14] (emphasis added):

13. In my judgment the law is as follows, having regard to the authorities. First, this court recognises that there are procedural and other restrictions legitimately placed upon solicitors and counsel alleging fraud. Fraud should not be asserted lightly. Second, if there is clear evidence of fraud, as Davis LJ made it clear, it must be clearly and unequivocally pleaded. Seeking to assert fraud by insinuation is not permitted and the pleading that makes such an insinuation must not and will not be sanctioned. Third, there is a clear line of well established case law (to which Cranston J referred) that establishes it is not necessary for a defence to make a substantive allegation of fraud or fabrication. If there are detailed facts from which the court (the trial judge) would be invited to draw an inference that the claimant has not in fact suffered the injuries or damage alleged, that may be pleaded. In other words, the defence have ammunition which is to be targeted at the claimant to undermine his case, such that he will be unable to prove the accident happened either at all or in the way that it is asserted. If that is the situation that may be pleaded.

14. In my judgment each case must turn on its own individual facts as to whether a case really is falling within the "fraud category" or the "sub-fraud category" in the way that I have just identified as the third point. A better label for that would be perhaps the "undermining ammunition category" or "inference category". In my judgment anyone assessing this situation has to decide whether the particular averment falls within the first or the second of those two categories. The answer is inevitably likely to be case and fact specific."

(1) Lorna Howlett (2) Justin Howlett v (1) Penelope Davis; (2) Ageas Insurance Limited [2017] EWCA Civ 696

The well-known case of *Howlett* was a claim in which the Second Defendant alleged that the collision was a low-velocity impact. In its defence, the Second Defendant pleaded that it did *"not accept the index accident occurred as alleged, or at all"* and required that the Claimants prove that they were *"involved in the index accident"*, that it was caused by the First Defendant's negligence, that they suffered injury and loss, and that such injury and loss were reasonably foreseeable. It further averred:

"If, which is denied, there was an accident as alleged, [Ageas] will aver that it was a low velocity impact unlikely to cause injury with injury being unforeseeable in any event."

The Defence went on to expressly indicate that the Claimants' credibility was in issue and asserted that they must prove their case on the balance of probabilities against the backdrop of particularly identified facts and/or contentions. The Defence then set out no fewer than 12 individual matters relied upon.

Most notably *Howlett* is a case dealing with issues concerning findings of fundamental dishonesty and is authority for the proposition that a Defendant does not need to plead a positive case of fundamental dishonesty in order for qualified one-way costs shifting to be displaced pursuant to CPR r. 44.16(1), provided such matters are properly explored in evidence and put to a witness in cross-examination so that he/she may deal with the allegation(s).

However, comments in the judgment of Newey LJ suggest an endorsement of the approach laid out in *Kearsley*. Certainly, there is nothing in his Lordship's judgment as a whole which would suggest that he considered the correctness of the approach advocated in *Kearsely* to be in question. Particularly, at [31], Newey LJ said (emphasis added):

> *"Statements of case are, of course, crucial to the identification of the issues between the parties and what falls to be decided by the Court. However, the mere fact that the opposing party has not alleged dishonesty in his pleadings will not necessarily bar a judge from finding a witness to have been lying: in fact, judges must regularly characterise witnesses as having been deliberately untruthful even where there has been no plea of fraud. On top of that, it seems to me that where an insurer in a case such as the present one, following the guidance given in Kearsley v Klarfeld, has denied a claim without putting forward a substantive case of fraud but setting out "the facts from which they would be inviting the judge to draw the inference that the plaintiff had not in fact suffered the injuries he asserted", it must be open to the trial judge, assuming that the relevant points have been adequately explored during the oral evidence, to state in his judgment not just that the claimant has not proved his case but that, having regard to matters pleaded in the defence, he has concluded (say) that the alleged accident did not happen or that the claimant was not present. The key question in such a case would be whether the claimant had been given adequate warning of, and a proper opportunity to deal with, the possibility of such a conclusion and the matters leading the judge to it rather than whether the insurer had positively alleged fraud in its defence."*

It therefore appears settled that the approach advocated in *Kearsley* remains good law, and should be followed by Defendants when pleading their Defence.

Practice Point 2: Disclosure and Identification of LVI as an Issue

The second important issue of practice arising from *Kearsley* pertains to the need to follow the relevant pre-action protocol, and to provide early, voluntary disclosure of documents. In particular, *Kearsley* advocates:

1. That claimant solicitors should offer the Defendant's insurer access to the Claimant's vehicle in order to facilitate an early examination, if so required.

   > Such an offer enables a Defendant insurer, if it considers it necessary, the opportunity to inspect the vehicle in its damaged state and take an early view as to whether a LVI defence is sustainable. If the damage to the Claimant's vehicle appears or transpires to be more than minor, such early inspection may well mean avoiding a LVI defence being raised at all. If those acting for a Claimant are satisfied that the damage to the vehicle is more than insignificant, it is difficult to see any obvious drawback in facilitating early inspection by the Defendant. It also shows a degree of candour and openness on the part of the Claimant – offering to let the Defendant insurance company inspect his/her vehicle shows that the Claimant has nothing to hide.

   > Such offers are not routinely accepted by the Defendant insurers (whether for logistical, timing, or other reasons). If the offer is made and the Defendant does not avail themselves of the opportunity but *later* produces engineering evidence which is based only on, for example, a desktop review of photographs of the Claimants' vehicle in its damaged state, that may provide the foundation for a reasonably powerful submission on behalf of the Claimant that the Defendant's evidence is far from satisfactory given they were afforded the opportunity to conduct an *actual* inspection but declined the invitation, and that the

Claimant's own expert evidence should therefore be prepared.

Obviously, such an offer will need to be made promptly; an offer to inspect an already repaired Claimant vehicle is likely to be of minimal, if any, real value.

From an objective standpoint, if the Defendant insurer does take up the opportunity to undertake an early inspection, and then seeks to rely on engineering evidence arising as a result of that inspection, the quality and usefulness of that evidence (to the Court) is likely to be significantly improved.

2. That claimant solicitors should voluntarily give early disclosure of any contemporaneous medical records.

Provision of such documentation will fall within the scope of the pre-action protocol. Experience suggests, however, that such records are not routinely provided by Claimant solicitors pre-issue, even in circumstances where a specific request for the records is made by a Defendant insurer in pre-action correspondence. In fact, it is not uncommon for reasonable requests for early provision of such records to be wholly denied or resisted. An unwillingness and/or failure to provide those records may well create difficulties later in the litigation and give rise to arguments about failures to comply with the letter/spirit of the pre-action protocol, and costs sanctions. A simple example highlights the potential issue: (i) a Defendant indicates that it intends to raise LVI as an issue, investigates on that basis, and requests the Claimant's relevant medical records but those records are not provided voluntarily; (ii) such records are only provided later in the litigation, post-issue; (iii) those records contain a number of entries demonstrating contemporaneous attendance by the Claimant at his/her GP, referring to the index accident and complaining of injuries consistent with those set out in the medical report(s); (iv) the records lead the Defendant to the conclusion that a LVI defence is unsustainable, and it is thus abandoned; (v) the case is settled. In such circumstances, the Defendant would have cogent arguments that the failure to provide early voluntary disclosure of the records led to an inability to properly consider the strength of a LVI defence; the unnecessary issuing of proceedings; and the avoidable incursion of costs. As practitioners we are constantly reminded by the higher courts that litigation should be seen as a last resort. In this hypothetical scenario, it would not be surprising if a costs sanction was visited on the Claimant.

Indeed, in *James Golden v Deborah Dempsey* (Manchester County Court) (1 December 2010) HHJ Holman was keen to emphasise the duty imposed on parties under CPR r. 1.3 to assist the Court in furthering the Overriding Objective, which includes co-operation, and the Judge gave guidance at [9] – [10] that in the majority of cases it ought to be perfectly possible to have completed disclosure and inspection on a voluntary basis before the issue of proceedings and certainly before the first directions hearing. In *Golden*, the Claimant's solicitor's failure to properly engage with the Defendant and to progress the case generally, including a refusal to provide medical records voluntarily, led to a costs sanction being imposed.

There does, however, have to be a degree of realism on both sides of the case. It has to be appreciated that there are, in the current climate, administrative difficulties in obtaining such records promptly (particularly where they have to be obtained from a number of different institutions). It is not uncommon to experience delays of two – three months (or longer) for records to actually be provided by the record holder, following a request for their provision. However, it is suggested that Claimant solicitors should seek to obtain those records as soon as practical upon instruction and, where possible, should avoid issuing/serving proceedings before those records are obtained and disclosed.

As with every personal injury claim there may well be entirely understandable concerns expressed by the claimant (and/or his advisers) in relation to data protection and confidentiality given the sensitive nature of such documentation. In that regard, the precise approach advocated in *Kearsley* is noteworthy: (i) the Court of Appeal referred specifically to the provision of *"contemporaneous GP"* or *"other relevant"* medical notes; the scope of the expected early disclosure is therefore reasonably limited: the Court does not appear to expect disclosure of the entirety of a claimant's medical records/history, only those documents proximate in time to the index events and/or those which are considered "relevant" (which might include, for example, historic, pre-accident entries relating to other neck, shoulder(s) and/or back injuries). A Claimant could reasonably refuse to provide any medical records which fell outside the ambit of those identified by the Court of Appeal; and (ii) the Court expressly indicated that the Claimant was at liberty to redact irrelevant passages within the medical notes – thereby ensuring that as much of the Claimant's confidential information as possible, remains confidential.

3. Defendant solicitors/insurers should indicate, in early course, that they consider the case to be low-velocity impact claim and they intend to investigate it as such.

    This guidance reflects the "cards on the table" approach required by the Civil Procedure Rules generally, and enables the parties to understand the landscape of the claim in early course and thus prepare accordingly and proportionately. It also means that relevant evidence, on both sides of the litigation, should be preserved. Further, it enables the court to accurately and actively manage the case from the beginning, thereby avoiding the need for interim applications and/or delays to the directions timetable; in doing so, the parties would be discharging their duty under CPR r. 1.3.

This particular point of guidance was further explained and amplified by the Court of Appeal in *Casey*, to which we now turn.

Debbie Casey v David Cartwright [2007] EWCA Civ 1280

Background

Casey concerned a case management appeal. The District Judge had granted permission for the parties to rely on the evidence of a joint expert on orthopaedic issues arising in the case. HHJ Holman, on a first appeal, revoked that permission. Permission to appeal was granted by HHJ Holman himself (unusually (given it was a case management decision) as the Court of Appeal noted) on the basis that he considered his decision raised important policy issues, particularly in light of the earlier decision in *Kearsley*.

The underlying facts were straightforward. The claim concerned a collision between two cars; the Defendant had hit the Claimant's vehicle in the rear. Liability was admitted. The Claimant's initial medico-legal expert concluded that she had sustained a soft tissue whiplash injury which, with the benefit of physiotherapy, would recover within nine months of the accident. The Defendant alleged that the incident was a low-velocity impact and indicated that causation was in issue. The Defendant's position was amplified in the Defence which pleaded that the accident was a very gentle incident; the speed of the Defendant's vehicle was around 2mph; and the forces transmitted from the Defendant's vehicle to the Claimant's vehicle were insufficient to cause personal injury to the Claimant.

The District Judge gave permission for a joint orthopaedic report to be obtained and allocated the claim to the Multi Track. A Mr Williams produced an orthopaedic report within which he noted there was a wealth of published evidence to the effect that at impact velocities of between 5 – 10mph, injury to the occupants of the struck vehicle was unlikely to occur and, if it did occur, it was likely to result in symptoms lasting no more than a few days because the forces directly attributable to the impact velocity are modified by the absorption of energy by the two vehicles upon impact with resultant velocity change in the struck vehicle. This was known as the "*v*". Mr Williams opined that the velocity change was approximately half the velocity impact. He concluded that on the balance of probabilities, the collision in *Casey* occurred at low velocity with a *v* of less than 5mph.

<u>Court of Appeal</u>

The Court of Appeal referred to the decision in *Kearsley*. The Court noted that the series of trials which had been envisaged in *Kearsley* had not taken place. Although some steps had been taken to facilitate that proposal, a consensus had been reached between McCombe J (as he then was) and the four Designated Civil Judges on the Northern Circuit, that it was not possible to identify suitable cases for the trial of generic issues – further investigation was required. The Court also noted that on 14th March 2005 McCombe J issued a Practice Note[11] with the approval of Dyson LJ and directed that, in order to achieve some consistency of approach pending authoritative decision, all applications to adduce expert evidence on issues of causation in low-velocity road traffic claims on the Northern Circuit should be issued/transferred to the relevant Designated Civil Judge.

---

[11] The Practice Note (as amended) was replaced by a similar Practice Note on 1/2/11 (a copy of which can be seen here: https://www.manchesterlawsociety.org.uk/2011/01/17/low-velocity-impact-road-traffic-claims/)

The Court of Appeal observed that HHJ Holman had given permission to appeal to *"enable the defendant to raise the wider issue as to the correct approach to the giving of permission to adduce expert evidence on questions of causation in low-velocity impact cases"* [22].

The Court of Appeal noted that it had already provided guidance as to the correct approach to the permissibility of expert evidence on causation in low-velocity impact cases in *Kearsley* (pending authoritative guidance in the anticipated test cases before a High Court Judge). The desirability of such test cases arose from the fact that the potential for a low-velocity impact to cause injury was a matter of some controversy, with some experts believing that one can never say definitively that below a certain '*v*' injury was impossible or even very unlikely; and other experts taking a different view and saying that below a certain '*v*' injury was impossible or, at any rate, very unlikely.

The Court noted that the guidance given in *Kearsley* had not assisted in achieving the degree of consistency of approach that had been hoped for and intended, and the guidance therefore needed to be amplified. In amplifying that guidance, the Court sought to emphasise that, *"...the further guidance that we propose to give is no more than that. Case management decisions are ultimately a matter for the discretion of the court. But it is undesirable that different courts should adopt different approaches to the same general problem. That creates more uncertainty than is necessary or justified"* [28].

At [30] – [37] the Court then provided the following guidance, which repays reading in full:

> *"30. We think that it is desirable that, if a defendant wishes to raise the causation issue, he should satisfy certain formalities. In this way, the risk of confusion and delay to the proceedings should be minimised. Accordingly, where in a particular case a defendant wishes to raise the causation issue, he should notify all other parties in writing that he considers this to be a low impact case and that he intends to raise the causation issue. For the reasons set out at [33] below, he should do so*

within three months of receipt of the letter of claim. The issue should be expressly identified in the defence, supported in the usual way by a statement of truth. Within 21 days of serving a defence raising the causation issue, the defendant should serve on the court and the other parties a witness statement which clearly identifies the grounds on which the issue is raised. Such a witness statement would be expected to deal with the defendant's evidence relating to the issue, including the circumstances of the impact and any resultant damage.

31. Upon receipt of the witness statement, the court will, if satisfied that the issue has been properly identified and raised, generally give permission for the claimant to be examined by a medical expert nominated by the defendant.

32. If upon receipt of any medical evidence served by the defendant following such examination, the court is satisfied on the entirety of the evidence submitted by the defendant that he has properly identified a case on the causation issue which has a real prospect of success, then the court will generally give the defendant permission to rely on such evidence at trial.

33. We believe that what we have just said reflects the tenor of the judgment in <u>Kearsley</u>. There will, however, be circumstances where the judge decides that, even though the evidence submitted by the defendant shows that his case on the causation issue has real prospects of success, the overriding objective nevertheless requires permission for expert evidence to be refused. It is not possible or desirable to produce an exhaustive list of such circumstances. They include the following. First, the timing of notification by the defendant that he intends to raise the causation issue. Unless the defendant notifies the claimant of his intention to raise the issue within three months of receipt of the letter of claim, permission to rely on expert evidence should usually be denied to the defendant. It is important that the issue be raised at an early stage so as to avoid causing delay to the prosecution of the proceedings. The period of three months is consistent with para.2.11 of the Pre-Action Protocol for Personal Injury Claims which provides that

a defendant be given three months to investigate and respond to a claim before proceedings are issued.

34. Secondly, if there is a factual dispute the resolution of which one way or the other is likely to resolve the causation issue, that is a factor which militates against the granting of permission to rely on expert evidence on the causation issue. In such a case, expert evidence is likely to serve little or no purpose.

35. Thirdly, there may be cases where the injury alleged and the damages claimed are so small and the nature of the expert evidence that the defendant wishes to adduce so extensive and complex that considerations of proportionality demand that permission to rely on the evidence should be refused. This must be left to the good sense of the judge. It does not detract from the general guidance given at [32] above.

36. We should say something about single joint experts. They have an invaluable role to play in litigation generally, especially in low value litigation. But we accept the submission of Mr Turner that, at any rate until some test cases have been decided at High Court level, judges should be slow to direct that expert evidence on the causation issue be given by a single joint expert. This is because the causation issue is controversial.

37. We repeat what we said at [36] of Kearsley about the desirability of having authoritative guidance by a test case or cases on the issue as soon as possible."

The appeal was ultimately dismissed.

Comment

The guidance given by the Court of Appeal is clear. It can be summarised thus:

1. Where a Defendant wishes to raise the causation issue it should:

    a. Notify all other parties *in writing* that it considers the claim to be a low-velocity case and that it intends to raise the causation issue. Such notification should be provided within three months[12] of the letter of claim;

    b. The issue should be expressly identified in the Defence. [In accordance with *Kearsley* the Defence should also plead those facts/matters/circumstances which the Defendant intends to rely upon at trial, in order to invite the Court to reject the Claimant's assertion that they sustained injury in the accident];

    c. Within 21 days of serving a Defence raising the causation issue, the Defendant should serve on the Court and the other parties a witness statement which clearly identifies the grounds on which the issue is raised. The statement should deal with the Defendant's evidence on the issue, including the circumstances of the impact and any resultant damage [to the vehicle(s)]. (The content of the relevant witness statement is likely to closely mirror, if not replicate, those matters already identified in the Defence).

---

12   A period consistent with the then Paragraph 2.11 of the Pre-Action Protocol for Personal Injury Claims, which provided a Defendant with 3 months to investigate and respond before proceedings were issued; and which remains consistent with paragraph 6.3 of the current PI Pre-Action Protocol.

2. If the Defendant follows all the steps in (1):

    a. Upon receipt of the witness statement the Court will, if satisfied the issue has been properly identified and raised, *generally* give permission for the Claimant to be examined by a medical expert nominated by the Defendant;

    b. On receipt of that medical report, if the Court is satisfied on the entirety of the evidence submitted by the Defendant (i.e. not <u>just</u> the medical report, but the medical report in conjunction with all the other evidence available) that the Defendant has properly raised a case on the causation issue that has a real prospect of success, the Court will *generally* then give permission for the Defendant to rely on the medical evidence at trial. [It is important to note that the guidance in *Casey* therefore anticipates a two-step process in relation to permission for expert evidence on behalf of the Defendant: (i) first, permission for the Defendant to *examine* the Claimant and have a report produced; and (ii) secondly, and <u>separately</u>, permission for the Defendant to *rely* on that report at trial].

3. However, even where the Defendant demonstrates that it does have a real prospect of success, there will be cases where the Overriding Objective dictates that permission for the Defendant to rely on its own medical evidence should be refused. They include (but are clearly not limited to):

    •   Where the Defendant fails to notify the Claimant of his intention to raise the issue within three months of receipt of the letter of claim. In such circumstances, permission should ordinarily be refused;

- Where the resolution of a factual dispute would likely resolve the causation issue – in such circumstances, expert evidence would likely serve little or no purpose; or

- The injury alleged and the damages are so small and the nature of the expert evidence so extensive/complex that considerations of proportionality demand that permission to rely on the evidence should be refused.

The Court of Appeal was clearly at pains to highlight that the judgment in *Casey* represented <u>guidance</u>, and no more than that. Dyson LJ's choice of language throughout the above paragraphs is instructive:

(a) When considering what approach the Court should adopt if the Defendant complied with the suggested steps, he twice employs the word "*generally*";

(b) When observing that (notwithstanding the Defendant's compliance with the suggested steps) there are circumstances when permission to rely on its own medical evidence should still be refused, he states that, "*It is not possible or desirable to produce an exhaustive list of such circumstances*". He continues that a failure to raise the issue within three months would mean that permission "*should **usually** be denied*"; that where there is a factual dispute which would likely resolve the causation issue this, "*is a factor which **militates against** the granting of permission*"; and that in considering issues of proportionality, although this may "*demand*" that permission to rely on the evidence should be refused, "*[T]his **must be left to the good sense of the judge**.*" (emphasis added throughout).

Throughout the judgment his Lordship uses the language of *flexibility*. The judgment recognises that the decision whether to grant permission for the Defendant to rely on its own medical evidence, or not, is inherently fact sensitive and case specific

In *Mirajuddin Molodi v (1) Cambridge Vibration Maintenance Service; (2) Aviva Insurance Limited* [2018] EWHC 1288 (QB), Martin Spencer J considered (at [40]) that, given the Defendants in that case were alleging that the collision was a 'low-velocity impact' it was "*unfortunate*" that the "*usual procedure*" in such cases was not pursed, with reference being made to the decision in *Casey*; comments which clearly demonstrate the continuing applicability of, and importance of complying with, the *Casey* guidelines.

It is suggested that unless there are <u>very cogent and sustainable</u> reasons preventing a Defendant from complying with the guidance given in *Casey*, it should be followed <u>precisely</u>. From a Defendant's perspective, where compliance *is* possible there is certainly no reason to run the risk that in due course the Court will refuse the desired permission simply because of a failure to follow the *Casey* guidance strictly. Claimant solicitors should be astute in relation to any failings to follow the *Casey* guidelines as it may be the platform for a successful defence to any application by the Defendant for permission to rely on their own evidence.

Perhaps one of the key messages from *Casey* is a reminder that the Civil Procedure Rules are sufficiently flexible to accommodate each case *individually*; it is therefore crucial when considering the prospects of successfully applying for permission to rely on their own expert medical evidence, that Defendant advisors look at the facts of each case in light of the Overriding Objective and through the prism of proportionality.

Of course, questions of permission for expert evidence are case management decisions and, absent any identifiable error of law, are extremely difficult to overturn on appeal; it is therefore important to get it right in the first instance.

CHAPTER FIVE

EXPERT EVIDENCE

In LVI cases the two most important sources of expert evidence come in the form of (i) engineering evidence; and (ii) medical evidence. Both have crucial roles to play in the proper investigation into, and determination of, LVI cases; although it should be noted that neither source of evidence is *necessarily* determinative of the outcome at trial[13].

(i)   Engineering Evidence

Engineering evidence falls into two main categories: (a) automotive assessor's reports; and (b) forensic engineering reports. The two usually serve different primary purposes and, accordingly, have different focuses/emphasises; they are also often written by differently qualified individuals. It is common to see both types of report utilised in LVI cases, but it is important to understand the scope, as well as the limitations, of each in order to ascertain which type of engineering evidence should be obtained to give the best chance of proving a claim, or defeating it on the basis of LVI.

Automotive Assessor's Report

In the first instance such reports are normally obtained by Claimants and served with the Particulars of Claim (if not provided beforehand in advance disclosure) in order to substantiate: (i) the fact of damage having been caused to the Claimant's vehicle; (ii) the location/areas of such damage; (iii) the magnitude of the impact (in broad terms); (iv) the roadworthiness, or otherwise, of the vehicle as a result of the collision; (v)

---

[13] See: *(1) Joe Armstrong; (2) Nicola Conner v First York* [2005] EWCA Civ 277 [dealt with in detail later in this work in Chapter 7]

the nature of repairs required to put the vehicle back into its pre-accident state, including a breakdown of necessary materials, repairs, and parts required; and importantly (iv) the cost of repairing the vehicle and; (v) whether the value of such repairs renders the vehicle an economic 'write off' or a repairable proposition.

It is suggested that the primary role of such reports is to prove the costs of necessary repairs and the pre-accident valuation of the Claimant's vehicle so as to enable the Claimant to claim either (i) the cost of such repairs as damages representing the diminution in value of the vehicle; or (ii) the pre-accident value of the vehicle where it is a 'write off'.

Often the engineer preparing the report will take photographs of the damaged vehicle. If they are not provided with the report they should be requested separately as they may be of particular assistance in gaining an impression of the nature and extent of damage caused.

The level of analysis in automotive assessor's reports is normally minimal. The engineer will usually simply state what in his/her opinion are the required repairs and the attendant costings, together with the pre-accident valuation of the vehicle based on some limited research (often of Glass's Guide).

Very often such reports are prepared following no more than a cursory visual examination. Experience also suggests that such visual examinations are undertaken reasonably swiftly, with engineers sometimes undertaking numerous such examinations of different vehicles on the same day or, at least, in a reasonably short space of time. The engineer usually does not thoroughly *inspect* the vehicle; it is almost unheard of for such examinations to include any dismantling of the vehicle. Certainly, it is not uncommon for the engineer to give his/her view as to, for example, the sums involved relating to labour charges for the repairs but with the express caveat that further damage may become apparent on dismantling/stripping the vehicle. In some senses, such reports are therefore preliminary in nature given it is possible the full extent of the damage incurred may only become apparent on closer and more detailed inspection of the vehicle; the reports have some inherent limitations in that regard.

Moreover, given the stage of the litigation at which such reports are ordinarily obtained (more often than not they are obtained pre-action by a Claimant, before LVI may even have been formally raised as an issue) they will invariably consider only the Claimant's vehicle. There will be no assessment of the Defendant's vehicle; no comparison between the two; and no commentary in relation to damage consistency.

Forensic Engineering Report

Defendants are likely to consider that they want to obtain a forensic engineer's report in cases where they wish to pursue a LVI defence. Experience tends to suggest, however, that in cases proceeding on the Fast Track many Judges have concerns in relation to the proportionality of granting permission for such evidence; it is thus often difficult to convince a Court that such evidence should be allowed. Moreover, Judges very often raise concerns about the usefulness of such evidence and whether, in accordance with CPR r. 35.1, it is 'reasonably required' to resolve the proceedings. Such concerns commonly stem from:

(a) An apprehension that such reports often lack any real quality or probity. Judges experienced in dealing with LVI cases will, no doubt, have seen many similar reports in the past. It is suggested that a significant number of such reports are poor in their preparation, lacking in substantive reasoning, and deficient in terms of their conclusions and opinions. In those circumstances, experience tends to suggest that Judges are reticent to grant permission for such evidence because of a perception that it is unlikely to make a material difference to the outcome at trial. Of course, such concerns ought not to lead the Court to dismiss an application for permission to rely on such evidence because each application should be decided on its own merits in the context of each individual claim. However, the fact of the concern ought to reinforce the need for Defendants to ensure that any such report for which permission is sought (if it is available when permission is requested) is properly prepared in accordance with Part 35; and

(b) A view that the Court is perfectly able to reach a safe conclusion on the issue of causation, and do justice between the parties, by hearing oral evidence from the respective drivers, having such evidence challenged by way of cross-examination, and considering the medical and other engineering evidence available.

If permission is granted to the Defendant, then the Claimant will no doubt want to instruct his/her own forensic engineer to ensure equality of arms; it is certainly arguable that there would be a 'mis-match' as between the author of an automotive assessor's report on the one hand, and a forensic engineering, on the other.

Forensic engineering evidence tends to consider, inter alia:

(i)   The nature and extent of damage to the Claimant's vehicle, together with costings for repair;

(ii)   The nature and extent of damage to the Defendant's vehicle, together with costings for repair;

(iii)   Whether the damage on the Claimant's vehicle is consistent with the damage caused to the Defendant's vehicle;

(iv)   Whether any damage visualised on either vehicle is likely to be pre-existing or otherwise non-accident related;

(v)   The likely speeds of the vehicles immediately prior to impact;

(vi)   The likely force transmitted from the Defendant's vehicle to the Claimant's vehicle as a result of the collision (bearing in mind the damage observed, the particular specifications of each vehicle's bodywork/bumpers etc., and on application of the laws of physics);

(vii)   The delta *v* experienced by an occupant of the Claimant's car;

(viii)   A layman's explanation of the likely force experienced by the Claimant (for example, in circumstances where the engineer concludes that the force transmitted to the Claimant was minor, it is sometimes said by the engineer that the forces imparted to the Claimant would be no greater than those experienced when pulling away from a traffic light, or stalling unexpectedly); and

(ix)   Whether occupant displacement of anyone present in the Claimant's car was likely to have resulted from the collision.

It might be argued that the last item on the above list is a matter that strays outside the proper remit of such expert evidence, and impermissibly ingresses into the factual findings the Court is required to make, although the point is clearly capable of debate.

Forensic engineering reports tend at least to *appear* to be more thorough and detailed in their analysis of the issues on which the expert is instructed to opine. Looks can, however, be deceiving. The fact that the forensic engineering report is a much fuller document does not necessarily mean that it will ultimately win the day at Court. In the first instance, one has to look closely at the underlying material forming the basis of the expert's opinion in order to consider whether the report and its conclusions are likely to withstand judicial scrutiny at trial.

Perhaps most importantly one has to consider whether the engineer has actually had the opportunity to inspect the Claimant's vehicle in its damaged state. Very often, by the time a forensic engineer is instructed, the Claimant's vehicle has been repaired, or sold (whether for scrap or otherwise) and is no longer capable of being physically inspected. This can present a real and significant limitation because the forensic expert is then required to rely on whatever material *is* available in order to assess the nature and extent of damage to the Claimant's vehicle. More often than not such material comprises: (i) the Claimant's initial assessor's report together with any photographs taken during that examination; (ii) any photographs and/or footage taken by either party at the scene or subsequently; and (iii) any written accounts by the Claimant and/or Defendant.

These indirect sources all have their limitations. Shortcomings inherent in a vehicle assessor's report are touched upon in the immediately preceding sub-heading. It should be noted that forensic engineering reports commonly include a significant focus on the state/condition of the rear bumper of the Claimant's vehicle because in most LVI cases, this is the part of the Claimant's vehicle which has sustained the relevant impact. However, modern day bumpers are designed in such a way as to absorb and redistribute the force of any impact from behind, in an attempt to minimise damage to the vehicle itself as well as any occupants, meaning that often the bumper deforms and reforms into its original shape. A cursory visual inspection of the bumper, as might well be undertaken by an assessor simply setting out costings for repairs, may not discover further or more extensive damage *behind* or *underneath* the bumper (whether to what is known as the reinforcement bar or "re-bar", or otherwise) and may therefore not accurately represent the full picture of damage actually caused to the Claimant's vehicle. Therefore, where the Defendant's *forensic engineer* is forced to rely on the Claimant's *vehicle assessor's* examination due to an inability to carry out his/her own physical inspection, the limitations in the latter's report, necessarily become inherent limitations in the former's report.

Reliance on photographs and/or footage in order to compile a forensic engineering report is useful up to a point but naturally they photographs/footage only show whatever can actually be visualised; they do not tell the whole story. Nor do such photographs/footage necessarily show the totality of damage sustained. That is particularly so in relation to any internal or structural damage in circumstances where all the photographs/footage are taken from outside the vehicle whilst it is in an unstripped state. Accounts from either driver are, of course, subjective and subject to all the common problems and limitations relatable to witness evidence generally, and the fallibility of memory.

Thus, if a Defendant knows, or suspects, that it will want to pursue a LVI defence, it should indicate, in early course, that it requires the Claimant's vehicle to be retained in its damaged state, and arrangements made for the Defendant to instruct its own engineer to inspect.

The same, of course, holds true in relation to inspection of the Defendant's own vehicle. Whilst, for obvious reasons, it is no doubt easier for the Defendant to arrange an inspection of his/her own vehicle in its damaged state, if that has not proved possible (for whatever reason) care must be taken when considering the cogency and persuasiveness of the underlying material forming the basis of the forensic engineer's opinion.

Furthermore, if the Defendant has not been able to carry out a physical inspection of the Claimant's and/or Defendant's vehicle, it is important that any photographs the engineer relies on to form his/her opinion are clear, good quality, colour copies. It is not uncommon to see very poor quality, grainy, badly reproduced photographs, taken from distance, and which might have been copied a number of times before they are provided to the expert, on which the forensic engineer is asked to base his/her opinion. That is likely to be unsatisfactory from the Court's perspective. The Court may well struggle to accept that the engineer had good enough material on which to form a reliable conclusion. Ideally, electronic copies of the originals should be obtained or, failing that, good quality colour copies of the originals.

As with all expert evidence the forensic engineer's report must be logically sound and be supported by sustainable reasoning; it must give cogent explanations for rejecting certain possibilities where it concludes that other potentialities are, on balance, to be preferred. Experience tends to suggest that Judges will not be slow in disregarding entirely, or attaching very little weight to, forensic engineering evidence where any obvious flaws are present in the methodology adopted or where the expert has failed to adequately support the reasoning for his/her conclusion(s).

It is likely that there will be inherent limitations on the expert's ability to reach reliable conclusions based on features of the Claimant him/herself, about which the expert may be unaware. As touched upon in the opening Chapter of this work, those will probably include:

- A Claimant's age;

- A Claimant's gender;

- A Claimant's previous medical history (both generally and in relation to spinal conditions specifically);

- A Claimant's general vulnerability to injury;

- Whether a Claimant was aware of the impending collision and/or whether he/she was braced at the point of impact, or not; and

- The precise position of a Claimant's head/neck at the point of collision.

Full and thorough instructions to the expert may, to a degree, minimise the uncertainty that such factors insert into the equation, but it is unlikely that they can be removed altogether.

(ii)   <u>Medical Evidence</u>

Medical evidence is likely to be obtained from a Consultant Orthopaedic, A&E, Spinal, or Trauma specialist, who probably has a particular interest in the causation of injuries in 'low velocity' situations.

Whether permission for such evidence is given will depend in large part on the Defendant having followed the guidance in *Casey* (although for the reasons given in Chapter 4, compliance with those guidelines will not axiomatically lead to permission being granted).

It is important that any medical expert instructed has access to the Claimant's relevant medical records so as to ensure he/she is fully appraised of any pre-existing condition(s) or relevant factors unique to the individual Claimant, which may have a bearing on the likelihood of injury having been sustained in the collision.

In circumstances where there are multiple Claimants all present in the same vehicle at the point of impact it is important that each individual Claimant is considered separately and carefully by the expert. Whilst injury may be inherently unlikely to one Claimant (for example because that Claimant was young, fit, otherwise healthy, and braced for the collision) the particular medical/physical characteristics/pre-dispositions of another Claimant might mean that he/she may well have, or indeed was likely to have, suffered injury in the collision (for example, because that Claimant was elderly, suffered with pre-existing degenerative change in the spine, and was unaware of the impending crash). It would be very unwise for any medical expert to treat each Claimant identically without descending into a consideration of their unique and differentiating features or, where no such features existed, without confirming that on careful review of the relevant medical records there were no entries of note distinguishing one Claimant's position from the other's.

Ideally, the medical expert should also be provided with: (i) the pleadings; (ii) the parties' witness statements (where available); (iii) all relevant engineering evidence (including good copy colour photographs) and (iv) any other medical reports arising as a result of previous or subsequent road-traffic accidents; as these documents may well inform the expert's overall conclusions, and the absence of consideration of some/all of them may well leave the expert's opinion open to challenge on the basis it failed to consider a relevant matter properly.

CHAPTER SIX

MEDICAL RECORDS AND FURTHER SOURCES OF EVIDENCE/INFORMATION

The previous Chapters of this work highlight the importance of:

1. An early, full conference with the client (probably with the assistance of Counsel);

2. The collation and retention of any photographic evidence; and

3. Obtaining and providing the Claimant's medical records in early course.

Claimant's Medical Records

Obtaining and reviewing the Claimant's medical records is an essential component of investigating and preparing a case in which LVI is raised in the Defence. It enables those involved in prosecuting or defending such cases to ascertain:

(a) Whether the Claimant had a relevant pre-accident history of injury and/or had been involved in other accidents (whether before the index accident, or subsequently). Such matters are relevant not only in relation to causation per se, but also in relation to the Claimant's consistency of reporting more generally, something which is often critical to his/her overall credibility and has an appreciable impact on the prospects of success of the claim (as dealt with in more detail later in this Chapter when considering other medico-legal reports, and in Chapter 7).

(b) Whether the Claimant attended at any medical institution(s) after the accident, or not. If the Claimant did not do so his/her advisors will want to know *why* that was the case particularly where, objectively speaking, the injuries complained of are more than minor/trifling in their nature and/or the impact of those injuries on the Claimant's day-to-day work/social life is more than *de minimis*. There may be a perfectly good explanation as to why the Claimant did not go to seek medical attention. For example, it is not uncommon for Claimant's to explain that they had suffered a previous whiplash injury following which they had visited their GP surgery, only to be told to take painkillers and undertake home exercises and, having been given that advice previously, they simply followed the same advice after the index accident as well. Nor is it unusual for Claimants to assert that they knew it would take two – three weeks to obtain a doctor's appointment at their GP surgery and they thought they would be recovered by that stage, so they never arranged an appointment. Nor indeed is unusual for Claimants to say that their GP surgery and their local A&E are very busy, and the Claimant did not think it was appropriate to divert scarce NHS resources for his/her injuries which, whilst appreciable, were objectively minor and which the Claimant anticipated would resolve quickly. Some Claimants are stoic and just 'get on with it'. Some Claimants do not like going to the doctors and/or have a phobia about doing so. Such explanations are no more than common examples, but they are all perfectly capable of being accepted by the Court. Much will depend on the individual circumstances of the case. The explanation for not attending must hold up to a degree of scrutiny, particularly in light of the Claimant's previously demonstrated behaviour when it comes to attending at their GP surgery and/or A&E, as well as the view the Court forms of them as an individual. If those acting for Claimants consider that the explanation is not persuasive, in light of the particular facts of the case, serious thought will need to be given as to why that is the case, and whether it damages the Claimant's prospects of success in the claim.

(c) Whether the records suggest that the Claimant is the sort of person who regularly seeks medical assistance from his/her GP and/or A&E and if so, for what sort of complaints. If the records suggest that, pre-accident, the Claimant was a frequent attender in relation to minor ailments like coughs, colds, sore throats, earaches etc. the fact that he/she did not attend after suffering what may, for example, be described as "severe" or "moderate" whiplash injuries, lasting a number of months, and which had an appreciable impact on his/her daily activities, may cause the Court a degree of concern. It would, at first blush, appear inconsistent that the Claimant would ordinarily attend for such minor matters, but failed to do so following what might be being presented as significant physical injury post-accident. Whether the Claimant's failure to attend for medical assistance post-accident suggests that injury may not have been sustained at all is a *relative* matter to be determined bearing in mind (i) the nature and frequency of pre-accident attendances, (ii) the severity and impact of the accident-related injuries alleged; and (iii) his/her explanation for the non-attendance. Such matters are, of course, nuanced; a Claimant may be able to credibly explain why he/she attended on previous occasions, but not in relation to the injuries arising from the accident. If, for example, the Claimant is someone who suffers badly with asthma and is prone to suffering from serious chest infections which regularly cause him/her to be hospitalised, attending for what might otherwise be considered a reasonably minor looking cough may make complete sense. The analysis has to be case specific looking at matters holistically.

(d) If the Claimant *did* attend at a medical institution(s) post-accident, the nature of the injuries he/she described at that time and whether his/her reporting is consistent with (i) the nature/location of injuries later alleged – whether in the Claims Notification Form; to the medico-legal expert; in a Schedule of

Loss; or in the Claimant's witness statement; and (ii) the timing of onset of symptoms given in other documents. The hope is that the Claimant has consistently reported both the nature and timing of his/her injuries. Experience suggests that complete consistency across all relevant documents is rare, however the Courts expect a *measure* of consistency in reporting[14] and its absence can often be fatal to the claim. Where the Claimant has inconsistently reported his/her symptoms, those acting for him/her will want to know why. It might be thought that a person injured by another's negligence would be able to recall reasonably well which parts of their body were injured as a result. Where, for example, the Claimant attended his/her GP a couple of days after the accident complaining of knee pain, but he/she then informed the medico-legal expert that he/she suffered significant pain, discomfort and stiffness in his/her neck, upper back and both shoulders, the difference in reporting cannot immediately be obviously reconciled. The starker the inconsistency, generally, the more difficult it is to simply explain it away. In some instances, the differences *can* be credibly explained. For example, it might be that the Claimant informed his/her own GP that he/she had neck pain, and then went on to tell the medico-legal expert that he/she had neck, upper back and shoulder pain; the explanation for the *arguable* increase in symptomology being that the upper back and shoulder pain was actually referred pain from the neck which started after a few days/some weeks. Such an explanation may well be completely credible. It is not unusual for Claimants to explain that they were initially unaware of particular injuries or pain because it was masked by a more severe pain elsewhere. Nor is it unusual for Claimants to explain that although they might have been suffering from a particular source of pain/discomfort at the time

---

[14] See: the well known dicta of Martin Spencer J in *Molodi v Cambridge Vibration Maintenance Service; Avivia Insurance Limited* [2018] EWHC 1288 (QB) at [44]

they went to see their GP or to A&E, they did not mention it because they considered it more minor than *another* injury from which they were also suffering and they were focused on obtaining help with the more serious injury. Timing is also important – if the Claimant alleges to have suffered "immediate" pain in his/her neck, it may be thought odd that it did not feature in the injuries described to a doctor at A&E the following morning. If, however, the Claimant asserts that the pain came on "a few days" after the accident, it may well not have been present at the time of the attendance at A&E and therefore his/her failure to mention such symptoms at that point would be totally explicable. Again, the explanation given has to be assessed in light of the entire background of the case and the Claimant's credibility.

(e) If the Claimant *did* attend at a medical institution(s) how the Claimant described the index accident taking place and/or at what speed and/or how he/she experienced the collision and/or whether an impression of its severity was conveyed to the treating medical practitioner. Such records only go so far – whilst the treating medical practitioner will take a history from the Claimant it is suggested that the clinician's focus is primarily on the Claimant's *injuries* and not on how the Claimant describes the collision happening; any such record is therefore likely to be reasonably brief/cursory and arguably of limited value. That being said, a contemporaneous account of the accident is helpful in ascertaining how the Claimant perceived the collision at the time. It may go to strengthen the Claimant's case if it is a consistent version of events to that advanced in the litigation; or it may go to undermine the Claimant if he/she described the accident as very minor but he/she now asserts that it was a significant impact. Of course the Claimant may be able to explain a version of events recorded in a medical note which is, on its face, inconsistent (or at least not entirely commensurate with the version of events advanced in the litigation) as being, for example, wrong recorded by the clinician or an account that the Claimant gave whilst in shock and therefore inaccurate or unreliable. All such explanations have to be considered in light of the circumstances of the case.

(f) If the Claimant *did* attend at a medical institution(s) how long after the accident he/she did so. If there is an appreciable gap between the accident happening/the reported onset of symptoms and the first attendance at a medical institution this may tend to suggest that the report of alleged injuries is not genuine, or that there may have been another causes of the injuries. This particular point should be considered in light of the Claimant's reporting of the onset and severity of his symptoms. Where there is a delay in seeking medical help, those acting for Claimant's will want to know why. Many of the observations made in paragraphs (b) – (d) above will be relevant when considering the Claimant's explanation for the delay.

(g) Allied to (f) above – if the Claimant *did* attend at a medical institution(s) whether he/she did so before or after the instruction of lawyers. The Claims Notification Form usually provides an obvious point in time at which it can be safely concluded the Claimant had instructed his solicitors to bring a claim for personal injury compensation. It is sometimes asserted by Defendants that, where the first attendance for medical assistance takes place *after* the instruction of lawyers, the attendance itself is prompted by the solicitors/litigation process in that the Claimant forms the view (whether independently, in conjunction with others, or on advice) that it would be objectively helpful to his/her case for there to be a record in his/her medical notes of an attendance at which injuries arising from the accident are reported. Of course, a Claimant will know whether this is, in fact, the reason for the attendance or not, but it would be prudent to discuss such matters with him/her. Where the attendance (or at least the first such attendance) took place before the Claims

Notification Form was sent, then it is unlikely that a Defendant can raise the point, certainly with any real force[15].

(h) If the Claimant *did* attend at a medical institution(s) whether the Claimant him/herself attributed the injuries he/she was then suffering to the accident, or whether an alternative cause was mooted or given. Clearly it would be relevant if the Claimant attended his/her GP complaining of neck pain which, at the time, he/she attributed to falling down a set of stairs a few days before; any suggestion that such symptoms were causally related to the accident would suffer an uphill struggle in relation to the issue of causation given the contemporaneous account contained in the records. Again, where there is any ambiguity or inconsistency as between the medical record(s) and the Claimant's account full instructions must be taken and analysed.

(i) If the Claimant complains of having suffered ongoing symptoms over a period of some months, whether he/she re-attended at any medical institution(s) for further input or help after the initial attendance. If the Claimant's account to the medico-legal expert and/or in their statement is of objectively appreciable injuries, whether in terms of pain and suffering and/or in relation to their impact on the Claimant's life, it might be thought odd that having previously attended for medical input, when the injuries did not recover, they did not return to seek further advice or medical attention. Again, the Claimant may be able to provide an adequate explanation for the non-attendance; any such explanation must be considered in light of all the other circumstances of the case. It might be argued by Claimants that, if anything, the failure to re-attend goes to the overall severity of injury/symptoms experienced (and the basis on which the Court

---

[15] Although it might still be suggested that the attendance was solely for the purpose of obtaining a helpful record in the medical notes, which could be relied on later in the litigation to support the assertion that injury was sustained.

will therefore assess the appropriate level of damages) rather than the fact of injury per se.

(j) Whether, if the Claimant *does not* attend for medical attention expressly related to the index collision at all post-accident, he/she *does* nonetheless attend during any prognosis period but for unrelated, other matters. Such situations are reasonably common. Where Claimants attend their GP/A&E etc. complaining of unrelated medical complaints but fail to attend in relation to the alleged accident related injuries, very often Defendants will argue that this is strong evidence that injury was not sustained because if the Claimant *had* been injured as alleged he/she would either have (i) attended to tell the doctor about it and obtain medical assistance – as he/she did do with this unrelated condition/issue; and/or (ii) mentioned the accident related injuries at the time of the consultation which took place. Again, the Claimant's explanation, and its cogency, are key. There is a balance to be struck: one has to balance the seriousness/triviality of the unrelated ailment the Claimant *did* attend for, with the seriousness of the injuries allegedly suffered in the index accident. The starker the contrast between the two injuries/complaints, the more it is likely the Claimant will be required to explain why he/she attended for the minor ailment but did not attend for the more serious accident injuries. Many of the points raised in paragraphs (b) and (c) above are relevant as to the Claimant's failure to make mention of the index accident related injuries. Particularly as regards (ii) (and the failure to mention the injuries at the time of the unrelated consultation) it is not uncommon for Claimants to explain that they did not raise the accident related injuries because GP appointments are very time limited and, often, a patient is only 'permitted' to raise one issue per appointment. Such explanations will resonate with most readers' real life experience; they are therefore capable of being accepted by the Court. However, such explanations do not overcome the failure to obtain an appointment specifically for the accident related injuries; in that regard, the observations at paragraphs (b) and (c) above are engaged.

In addition to photographs and medical records, there are other potentially important sources of evidence/information available to both Claimants and Defendants which should be investigated, as they may well inform the likely prospects of success of a LVI defence.

Other Records

In addition to the medical records there may be other records, both of a medical and non-medical nature, which may go to support the Claimant's case that he/she was suffering from the effects of injury caused in the accident and which therefore can and should be obtained to bolster his/her claim. From a Defendant's perspective, the production of these documents may mean there needs to be an objective re-assessment of the prospects of a LVI defence.

Such records might include:

(i) Privately paid for treatment – this could be, for example, physiotherapy; osteopathy; acupuncture; massages; hydrotherapy. If the Claimant can demonstrate that he/she paid out of his/her own pocket for such services, ideally through the production of invoices or a letter from the treating practitioner, then this may be powerful evidence that the Claimant was, in fact, injured – it is suggested that a Court would find it inherently unlikely that an individual would go to the expense of paying for such treatment out of their own pocket if they were not actually injured. Of course, Defendants will want to ascertain whether such treatment(s) were being undertaken prior to the index accident in any event, for other unrelated ailments, such that it might be suggested that the treatment related to a pre-existing condition(s) and not any injuries arising in the accident;

(ii) Gym/other sporting records – if the Claimant was an active sportsperson prior to the accident, for example, if he/she attended the gym regularly, or attended a weekly yoga class, or played 11-a-side football every weekend for a local team etc.; if he/she was unable to engage in those regular activities because of ongoing symptoms caused by the accident this, too, is powerful evidence of injury having actually been sustained. Those acting for Claimants in such cases should consider obtaining online gym records; or letters/witness statements from those organising the activities and/or teammates, confirming the absence of the Claimant and, where possible, also confirming that the reason given by the Claimant for his/her absence was injury sustained in the accident. Particularly if the Claimant is a member of a club/team who arrange their activities by some electronic means, for example, confirming who is available to play in Saturday's upcoming game by email or Whatsapp message, it might be that the Claimant contemporaneously responded indicating he/she could not attend due to injury *arising from* the accident. Such communications should be obtained as this would be very persuasive evidence to put before the Court;

(iii) Employment records – if the Claimant asserts that he/she was absent from work as a result of the injuries sustained, it will be very helpful to obtain confirmation of that fact from his/her employer. This may include production of the employer's internal absence/sickness register and/or provision of a letter (or ideally) witness statement from the relevant individual at the Claimant's work. Again, if that individual can give evidence to the effect that he/she knew that the Claimant was off work and the reason the Claimant had given for that absence was the ongoing effects of injury which the Claimant explained were caused by the road traffic accident, that is likely to be particularly persuasive evidence. If the account can be supported by Med3 certificates from the Claimant's GP, so much the better.

CUE Searches and Prior Accidents

The Claims and Underwriting Exchange ("CUE") is a central database holding millions of records relating to car, home, travel and personal injury insurance claims and notifications. It includes all incidents reported to insurance providers, no matter how trivial, and irrespective of whether a claim is subsequently made. It is managed by the Motor Insurers' Bureau ("MIB"). Insurers supply the CUE database with information so that a record of an individual's claim and notification history is readily accessible. The CUE database was set up in 1994 to enable insurance companies to share information and help identify and combat insurance fraud. The CUE database can be accessed at: www.cuecheck.com

Practically all Defendant insurers have access to the CUE database and are able to interrogate its entries. Such information is likely to be of interest to Defendants considering running a LVI defence. First, a particular Claimant's claims history may be informative in relation to his/her propensity to bring claims for compensation arising out of road traffic accidents, or personal injury claims more generally. Secondly, although the information on the CUE database may be limited, it is possible that it will provide an indication as to the gravity/seriousness of the earlier accident(s), and may therefore shed some light on whether or not the Claimant has been involved in any previous LVI type cases. Thirdly, it is likely to show whether the Claimant's previous injury claims were settled, disposed of at trial, or abandoned by the Claimant. Such knowledge is likely to provide a springboard for Defendants to seek further information from the insurer(s) involved in those earlier cases and to query whether there were any concerns raised about the nature of the collision or the injuries suffered. Fourthly, it enables a Defendant to assess the veracity of the Claimant's reporting to their own medical expert(s) in the index claim, and whether the Claimant has correctly reported the number of previous incidents causing injury in which he/she has been involved. As a consequence, the Defendant may well have grounds to request disclosure of any medical reports created for the purposes of any previous claim. However, interrogation of the CUE database may also reveal to a Defendant that the Claimant has no, or no relevant, claims history, which may alleviate any suspicions as to the genuineness of the claim which the Defendant harbours. Secondly, it may indicate that, even if the Claimant has been involved in previous accidents, these were of a different character/nature and/or were not considered to be questionable or suspicious by the insurer(s) involved in that claim(s). Thirdly, it may go to show that the Claimant was entirely honest when reporting his/her previous accident history to their medical expert in the index claim. Any, or all, of those matters may lead the Defendant to re-assess the position and conclude that a defence of LVI looks less sustainable.

Whilst Claimant solicitors may not have access to the CUE database, there are two obvious avenues through which they can seek to obtain the information relating to the Claimant, which is held by the database. The first is for the Claimant to make a Subject Access Request him/herself; such a request can be made using the form on the MIB website (found here: https://www.mib.org.uk/media/425181/data-subject-access-request-cue_v20.pdf). The second is to request disclosure of such documentation from the Defendant given it is likely the Defendant's insurer will have obtained such information as part of its initial investigation. It is advisable that a Claimant's advisors obtain the documentation themselves in the first instance, to avoid any potentially unwelcome or unexpected surprises later in the litigation.

Other Medico-Legal Reports from Prior or Subsequent Accidents

It is important that those acting for Claimants properly investigate whether the Claimant has been involved in any previous or subsequent accidents (RTA or otherwise) and if so, whether he/she sustained any injury in those accidents. The information held by the CUE database will be able to assist in that regard but should not be considered a substitute for taking full instructions from the Claimant on the point, not least because the information on the CUE database is likely to be much more limited than that which the Claimant will be able to provide him/herself.

The purpose of looking into these matters is, essentially, twofold:

(a) To ascertain whether there are any injuries/symptoms from other accidents which may have a direct bearing on the causation of injury in the instant case; and

(b) To ascertain the consistency of the Claimant's reporting – to his own solicitors, to the medico-legal expert instructed in the case, and to the Defendant – as regards: his involvement in other accidents; if there were such accidents whether the Claimant was injured in those accidents; and if he/she was injured, the nature and extent of the injury, including the prognosis for recovery.

The nature and extent of any injury sustained[16] in a prior or subsequent accident may be directly relevant to the issue of causation in the immediate claim. For example, if the claim being brought is one for soft tissue/whiplash type injuries to the neck and upper back, it would be highly relevant that the Claimant had been involved in another RTA just two months beforehand, in which he/she also suffered a whiplash injury to his/her neck and/or upper back and in relation to which a medico-legal expert instructed in respect of that earlier accident had opined that it would take a total of six months for the Claimant to recover fully. Of course, in such circumstances the Claimant was likely still suffering from the effects (at least to some degree) of the earlier accident and therefore the symptoms present post index accident are unlikely to be completely causally related to the index collision. Similarly, if the Claimant is involved in an accident just one month later in which he/she sustains injuries to his/her neck and/or upper back, then this may cut short the period of suffering and/or the extent of symptoms, which can be causally related to the index accident.

However, and perhaps more importantly, obtaining and reviewing other medico-legal reports enables an assessment of the *consistency* of the

---

[16] As opposed to simply the fact of injury having been suffered.

Claimant's reporting. It might, for example, be considered by the Court to be highly relevant if the Claimant failed to disclose to the current medico-legal expert that he/she had been involved in a number of prior RTAs in which he/she sustained whiplash type injuries.

If the Claimant has been involved in any number of previous accidents which are not referenced in the expert's report, a number of obvious questions arise:

(a) Was the Claimant actually asked about previous accidents and/or the injuries sustained in them, by the expert, at the time of the examination?

(b) If so, did the Claimant fail to inform the expert about those other accidents and/or injuries? Or, as is sometimes asserted by Claimants, did the Claimant tell the expert about those matters and the expert has unfortunately failed to record them in the report or alternatively, attempted to record what the Claimant actually said but has done so inaccurately?

(c) If the Claimant did fail to disclose such matter(s) to the expert, why did he/she so fail? Was it an innocent mistake and/or forgetfulness and/or a failure to appreciate the relevance of the information not disclosed? Other explanations are naturally possible. Or did the Claimant, perhaps, deliberately withhold such information from the expert, so as to give a misleading impression of his/her physical condition immediately prior to the collision?

It is suggested that an appreciable number of cases fail at trial because the Claimant's reporting to a medico-legal expert in relation to his/her previous accident history and/or previous injury history can be shown to be inaccurate, incomplete or, in some cases, even dishonest, when it is compared with accounts contained in other medico-legal reports prepared in respect of other accident claims. That is so both in relation to:

(a) The reports prepared for the index claim – if the Claimant did not tell the expert about other prior and/or later accidents (which took place post-index accident but before examination) and their effects; and also

(b) Any reports prepared for later claims – if the Claimant failed to tell a later medical expert instructed for a subsequent accident, about the fact of the immediate claim and its effects, the Court is likely to take a dim view of his/her credibility as a witness.

Claimants who do not give open, full and accurate disclosure of their previous accident and/or injury history, whether to their medico-legal expert or in their witness statement, and who can be shown through the production of *other* medico-legal reports to have been inaccurate or less than forthcoming in relation to such matters, generally seriously damage their overall credibility by making such inaccurate or incomplete statements. Credibility, both of the Claimant him/herself and of their account more generally, is a highly relevant factor for the Court when considering whether the claim has been proved against a backdrop of a LVI defence. Sometimes the inconsistency of reporting is so damaging as to be fatal to the whole claim.

Medico-legal reports are of critical importance in personal injury claims. It is suggested that where an individual is willing and prepared to attend a medico-legal examination in order for a report to be prepared to support a claim for compensation, it is likely that the Court will consider (within reason and subject to any explanation(s) for any inconsistencies, omissions or errors) that what the Claimant told the expert at the time of examination was true, accurate and thorough; the report's contents are therefore highly probative as regards his/her consistency of reporting.

Obtaining any other medical reports which were commissioned in respect of previous and/or subsequent accidents enables an appraisal of whether the Claimant has been forthright in his/her reporting to the expert and to his/her own solicitors, both as regards involvement in any other accident(s), and also as regards the nature and extent of any injuries sustained in any other accident(s).

Whilst some failures of disclosure by the Claimant can probably be explained (for example, the Claimant may have only been involved in one previous RTA some 20 years ago in which he/she sustained very minor injuries which resolved quickly and he/she says that they simply forgot all about it when questioned by the medico-legal expert), others probably cannot (like an earlier RTA just two months prior in which identical injuries were sustained). The closer in time between the incident which the Claimant failed to disclose and the examination by the expert, the less likely it is that the Court will accept the Claimant simply forgot about it. The more serious the other accident and/or its injuries, the less likely the Court will accept that the Claimant simply forgot about it or did not think it was relevant. The more similar the injuries sustained in an earlier accident are to those allegedly suffered in the index accident, the less likely the Court will accept that the Claimant did not think it was relevant to disclose the fact of the accident and/or the injuries sustained. Whilst the immediately preceding statements are useful 'touchstones', naturally, all of these issues are case sensitive and have to be considered in light of the unique facts of each claim.

It is important to understand the Claimant's explanation for the non-disclosure of his/her involvement in those other accidents, and/or his/her failure to mention that he/she was injured in those accidents, as well as to objectively assess the veracity and cogency of that explanation. In doing so those acting for Claimants have an opportunity to satisfy themselves as to the prospects of success of the claim generally. Moreover, identifying these matters in early course enables full and detailed instructions to be taken from the Claimant. Such matters cannot be overlooked or brushed aside – they provide fertile ground for cross-examination at trial and therefore need to be considered and, where possible, neutralised in advance. This may include discussing the content of the medical report with the relevant expert and requesting (where appropriate) for any necessary corrections/revisions to be made, for example, if it is considered a mistake has been made, or something material mentioned by the Claimant at the time of examination has been omitted from the report, the expert can be asked to address such matters. Of course, the final content of the report is a matter for the expert him/herself in compliance with his/her duty of independence owed to the Court. Or, addressing such matters in advance may include dealing with them in the Claimant's own witness statement. A balancing act has to be struck. On the one hand obvious inconsistencies or problems should not be ignored – it is highly unlikely that the Defendant's advisers will fail to notice such issues and they will inevitably seek to rely on them at trial; indeed they may have already been expressly pleaded in the Defence. It is better for the Claimant to be on the 'front foot' in that respect and thereby seek to regain control of the narrative. Moreover, the Court is likely to be more accommodating or sympathetic to a Claimant who has dealt with such issues head on rather than simply ignore them, pretending they do not exist or are of no relevance; doing so shows a degree of candour and openness with the Court. On the other hand, seeking to deal with each and every small, minor, or potentially tangential inconsistency may give the Defendant more ammunition for trial which they were not initially intending to deploy. In each case a judgment call needs to take place as to whether an inconsistency is sufficiently problematic that it requires specific attention, or whether it can be left to trial for the Claimant to explain from the witness box.

Ultimately, if the Claimant's explanation makes little sense or is incredible (in the true sense of the word) then those acting for Claimants will need to consider why and in what respects the explanation is lacking; whether the explanation is so deficient or unbelievable that the claim no longer has any prospects of success; whether the claim should continue to be prosecuted at all and, finally, it will provide an opportunity for appropriate advice to be given to the Claimant in early course.

Social Media

It is highly probable that the Claimant has one or more social media accounts. This might be, for example, Facebook, Twitter, Instagram, TikTok etc. Many people, particularly those of a younger age, may have more than one account. As is well known, privacy settings on social media accounts vary from 'open' so that any member of the public can see and access the totality of the account and all its content; to 'closed' where, ordinarily, only people who are "friends" or in some way 'connected' to that individual can see his/her activity.

The frequency and manner in which different individuals use social media accounts varies widely. Some individuals post seemingly all aspects of their life on their social media account, sharing even mundane day to day moments with their followers. Others use social media to present a particular type of lifestyle in an attempt to cultivate a specific image. Others still post little if anything and simply use the platform to view others' content. Of course, there are many other gradations of usage between the examples stated.

Where the Claimant has an 'open' social media profile it is possible for the Defendant's advisors to review his/her posts/entries. Such posts/entries may provide useful evidence demonstrating what the Claimant was doing (and thus capable of doing) during the prognosis period of any supposed injury. Thereby the posts *may* suggest that the Claimant was not suffering from the injuries claimed. If, for example, the Claimant alleged that he was a competitive badminton player and he had been unable to play badminton since the accident because he had suffered a significant whiplash injury to his right shoulder, but he was posting weekly updates of his badminton training and competitions on Facebook, that might tend to suggest that there was no injury sustained and would be powerful evidence to place before the Court in support of a LVI defence.

CHAPTER SEVEN

SUCCESS OR FAILURE
AT TRIAL

Without wishing to state the obvious, in a LVI case the Court will take into account all of the evidence available in determining whether, on the balance of probabilities, the Claimant has discharged the burden of proving that he/she did sustain injury in the accident, and the nature and extent of such injuries. The types and significance of those different sources of evidence have been discussed in the earlier Chapters of this work. Each case will naturally turn on its own facts and the weight or importance to be attributed to a particular source or species of evidence will vary from case to case. It may well be in a particular case that no one, single piece/source of evidence is determinative of the outcome at trial. However, what can be said with certainty is that in <u>every</u> case the Claimant's credibility has an important role to play in determining whether the claim succeeds or fails. It is suggested that it is likely to be the key factor in most, if not all, cases.

The importance of the role a Claimant's credibility plays in LVI cases is most neatly demonstrated in the case of *(1) Joe Armstrong; (2) Nicola Connor v First York* [2005] EWCA Civ 277.

Claimant's Credibility: *Armstrong; Connor v First York* [2005] EWCA Civ 277

Facts

The claim arose out of a road traffic accident in which both Claimants said they had suffered soft tissue injuries to their spines as a result of hyper-extension/hyper-flexion. The Claimants' case was that they were travelling in a Ford Fiesta and were stopped at a red traffic light at crossroads in the city centre of York; they were away for the weekend and staying in a hotel. They were intending to turn right. Mr Armstrong was driving and either had his foot on the footbrake or his handbrake on. Mr Smith, the Defendant's bus driver, thought he could squeeze his bus down the nearside of the Claimants' car, but as he passed, he caused it a glancing blow to its rear nearside corner. The damage to the Claimant's car was minor – a scratch on its rear nearside panel which was 5 inches long and 200 microns deep which, the Judge at first instance, HHJ Stewart QC, said was double the normal thickness of paint. The Judge considered that on any view it was a very shallow scrape.

Trial

The issue at trial was, *"whether the forces generated by the impact were sufficient to jolt them* [the Claimants] *in their seats"* (at [3]) – a classic LVI case. HHJ Stewart QC found in favour of both Claimants and awarded them both a modest sum of damages.

A single joint expert[17], Mr Childs, had been instructed by the Claimants and Defendant and he was *"...of the clear view that no occupant displacement ... could have occurred as a result of the impact"* (at [4]). Mr Childs was asked Part 35 Questions and attended trial to give oral evidence.

The Judge found that the bus was probably driving at 10 – 15mph and the bus driver only braked after impact.

---

[17] It is suggested that, in the overwhelming majority of instances, the use of a single joint engineering expert is likely to be considered undesirable by both parties in LVI cases and, it is further suggested, that if the issue is raised appropriately by the Defendant, it is likely both parties will (subject to proportionality considerations) be granted permission for their own engineering evidence. It is likely that the Defendant may have already commissioned such evidence in advance of pleading a LVI defence, so the prospect of a single joint expert is further reduced as it would result in unnecessary duplication of work.

The Judge further found that the Claimants had felt pain during the course of their weekend in York and that on their way back to Liverpool they went to the hospital at Ormskirk where they were documented as complaining of pain. The Claimants were told that there would be a long wait to be seen. They did see the triage nurse who suggested that they saw their GP the following day instead of waiting in A&E, which they both did.

Both Claimants were examined for the purposes of medico-legal reports and provided witness statements; across those documents they both described how they were moved by the impact and the nature of the collision, describing it as a "bump". The Court of Appeal noted, "*They were giving a consistent story*" (at [12]).

The trial Judge considered the evidence of Mr Childs. It is worth noting the effect of his evidence, and the basis on which he had been able to report. The Judge recorded that, "*the effect of his evidence… was that there was minor damage to the bumper and the rear nearside panel of the Ford Fiesta, but not much more than a paint mark on the bumper and a scratch on the panel. There was also some very minor damage to the bus*" (at [13]). Mr Childs was "*reporting on the basis of what he had been told about the damage to the bus and an inspection that had been made on his behalf of the Ford Fiesta after repairs had been carried out.*" (at [14]).

Mr Childs' evidence was (at [14]):

"*… in order for the Fiesta to move just on its springs, without the vehicle's wheels moving, the impact would have had to be such as to cause some distortion to the panels of the vehicle, but there was not any. But if there was no distortion to the panels of the vehicle and the vehicle did not even move on its springs, there would be no movement of the occupants of the vehicle, much less any movement which could possibly injure their spines. Mr Childs said that unless the person in question is particularly vulnerable the vehicle would have to move on the road surface in order to cause injury. There was no evidence that this vehicle* *had moved across the road surface at all with either the footbrake or the handbrake on ".*

Importantly (in the context of the claim and the appeal), HHJ Stewart QC found that Mr Child's *"thesis"* stood up to questioning.

At trial, reliance was placed on the Court of Appeal's decision in *Cooper Payen Ltd v Southampton Container Terminal Ltd* [2003] EWCA Civ 1223[18], in particular the supporting judgment of Lightman J at [66] – [67] in which, of particular interest, his Lordship stated:

> *"67 Where a single expert gives evidence on an issue of fact on which no direct evidence is called, for example as to valuation, then subject to the need to evaluate his evidence in the light of his answers in cross-examination his evidence is likely to prove compelling. Only in exceptional circumstances may the judge depart from it and then for a good reason which he must fully explain. **But if his evidence is on an issue of fact on which direct evidence is given, for example the speed at which a vehicle was traveling at a particular time, the situation is somewhat different. If the evidence of a witness of fact on the issue is credible, the judge may be faced with what, if they stood alone, may be the compelling evidence of two witnesses in favour of two opposing and conflicting conclusions. There is no rule of law or practice in such a situation requiring the judge to favour or accept the evidence of the expert or the evidence of a witness of fact. The judge must consider whether he can reconcile the evidence of the expert witness with that of the witness of fact. If he cannot do so, he must consider whether there may be an explanation for the conflict of evidence or for a possible error by either witness, and in the light of all the circumstances make a considered choice which evidence to***

---

[18] Considered recently, seemingly without criticism, by the Court of Appeal in *Griffiths v TUI* [2021] EWCA Civ 1442 [a case which is, itself, subject to an appeal to the Supreme Court].

accept. The circumstances may be such as to require the judge to reach only one conclusion." (emphasis added)

At trial HHJ Stewart QC said that, *"so far as he knew, they* [the Claimants] *were of blameless character and that they gave their evidence in a transparently truthful, honest and guileless way"* (at [6]). He further stated,

> *"...before I heard Mr Childs' evidence, I did not for one moment consider that there was any possibility that either of these two witnesses were lying, were misleading me or had made up this claim. Not one jot of evidence, not one shred, seriously undermined (I emphasis 'seriously' because there were minor imperfections to which I have referred) my confidence in their veracity and straightforwardness. That was the clear and unequivocal impression which I formed of them in the witness box and which, albeit that of course a person may and does make mistakes in evaluating witnesses, I feel very confident in stating.*
>
> *Equally, Mr Childs gave his evidence in a way which was logical and consistent and there is some force in Mr Grant's* [Counsel for the Defendant] *criticism that the claimants have not called or applied to call any engineering evidence from another expert, in which case, according to Mr Grant, the defendants would not have objected."*

The Judge considered that the evidence of the Claimants and of Mr Childs could only be reconciled if (a) he found the Claimants were lying; or (b) he found that there was, in Mr Childs' evidence, the potential that there had been some error which has not been detected before the Court and to which the Court could not point.

The Judge noted that, *"...there are a number of cases in which this particular issue of low velocity impacts not being capable of causing injury are in the offing, and each case must be decided on its evidence and on the merits. There is no golden thread running through each case".*

HHJ Stewart Q.C. rejected the suggestion that because there was no discernible flaw in Mr Childs' evidence the Court was forced to conclude that the Claimants were liars. He considered that the Claimants were both honest and that there must, accordingly, be something which was not accurate in Mr Childs' evidence, which the Judge could not identify. He could not, "...*reconcile the evidence of the expert witness of fact. I can only say that there must be a possible error in Mr Childs' evidence, and I make a considered choice because of my clear and unequivocal impression of the claimants as witnesses*".

Court of Appeal

The Appellant argued that Defendants should be entitled to rely on the evidence of an accident reconstruction expert of Mr Childs' quality and once it had been tested in Court and found to 'come up to proof', that should be the end of the case. Criticism was made of the Claimants' decision not to call an expert of their own to deal with the issue. It was argued that Mr Childs' evidence was dispositive of the case.

Brook LJ giving the judgment of the Court of Appeal stated, at [26] – [28]:

> "*[26] In my judgment, in this very difficult case the judge directed himself correctly as a matter of law. He was entitled to consider the evidence he had been given by the claimant extremely carefully, directing himself about the dangers of witnesses who may seem to be very plausible but in fact are telling a pack of lies, and directing himself to consider very carefully the evidence given on behalf of the defendant. He formed the view that he could not be satisfied that these witnesses were telling a pack of lies. He was very impressed by their evidence, and he concluded, when he had to balance the evidence of each side, that there must be – although he accepted fully that he could not say what it was – something which was not accurate in Mr Childs' evidence in this particular case.*
>
> *[27] In my judgment there is no principle of law that an expert's evidence in an unusual field – doing his best, with his great experience, to reconstruct what happened to the parties based on the secondhand*

material he received in this case – must be dispositive of liability in such a case and that a judge must be compelled to find that, in his view, two palpably honest witnesses have come to court to deceive him in order to obtain damages, in this case a small amount of damages, for a case they know to be a false one.

[28][...] In the last resort it is for the judge – or it may be the jury in a criminal trial as the triers of fact – to determine, on the balance of probability, on all the evidence they receive, where the probabilities lie. It may be that they are impelled to that conclusion when they are weighing two different types of evidence, one from extremely honest appearing witnesses of fact and the other from an expert doing his best in his particular field of expertise".

Brooke LJ did not consider dismissal of the appeal would lead to a raft of dishonest claimants seeking damages because *"in very many cases"* the evidence of a witness like Mr Childs may very well be sufficient to tip the balance strongly in favour of the Defendant (at [29]).

In a concurring judgment, Longmore LJ stated (at [35]), *"If a judge is convinced, on proper evidence, that the claimants are in fact telling the truth and are not fraudulent, that conviction may well be a reason for declining to accept expert evidence to the contrary effect".*

The appeal was therefore dismissed.

Comment

In *Armstrong*, the expert evidence was clear – the Claimants could not have been injured because the collision was, by its nature, incapable of having caused occupant displacement. That evidence was found to be logically sound, and the Court could not identify any error contained within it. Even though that was the position, the trial Judge had been entitled to prefer the Claimants' evidence and find that the claims had been proven because they presented as truthful, honest, consistent and reliable witnesses, and their account was not 'seriously' undermined in cross-examination. The case is a very clear example of the importance of the Claimant's own credibility in LVI cases – sometimes it is powerful enough to even overcome flawless expert evidence.

It is notable that HHJ Stewart Q.C. sought to stress that the Claimants' evidence had not been "seriously" undermined; there were it seems "minor imperfections" in their evidence which are, to some extent, perhaps to be expected or can be forgiven. It is not difficult to see how the outcome of the case may well have been different had the Claimants not stood up to cross-examination so well.

A robust conference with the Claimant is likely to be the best way to assess his/her likely credibility at trial although, as every litigator knows, the unique pressures of the Courtroom and the actual day of trial cannot be completely replicated in advance.

Other Common Reasons for Failure

As already set out, the Court will look at the totality of the evidence in determining whether the Claimant has discharged the burden of proof in relation to causation of injury. Each case will turn on its own facts and the actual evidence produced at trial. As HHJ Stewart Q.C. said in *Armstrong*, *"each case must be decided on its evidence and on the merits. There is no golden thread running through each case"* (emphasis added).

Any attempt to compile a comprehensive list of reasons why claims otherwise fail at trial would be a futile exercise. Apart from issues solely relatable to credibility, the following represent some additional common reasons as to why claims fail, or LVI defences are dismissed at trial:

(a) The absence or quality of the Defendant driver.

In many cases there will be a stark difference of account as between the two drivers in relation to the speed or magnitude of the impact. Of course, the Defendant driver's own credibility is engaged and if the Court considers that he/she is a credible witness who has given an account of a very minor coming together of two vehicles, this would be very persuasive evidence. The converse if obviously true – if the Defendant's driver is a poor witness and the Claimant a credible one, it is likely that the Court will accept the Claimant's version of events in relation to the magnitude of the collision and, probably, therefore accept the Claimant was injured. If, however, the Defendant driver has not provided a witness statement at all, or has provided a witness statement but fails to attend trial, it is very difficult to effectively challenge the Claimant's account as to the nature of the impact and the forces involved.

(b) A description of an incident given by the Claimant, which is out of all proportion to the damage sustained.

It is not uncommon for Claimants to subjectively describe what appears to be a rather severe collision. This description may have been to the expert, in their witness statement, or it may be something established in cross-examination (it can sometimes be useful to ask the Claimant to describe the severity/magnitude etc. on a scale of 0 – 10). It might be, for example, that they describe a significant shunt of one or more car lengths etc. It may also be that during the course of their oral evidence the Claimant actually seeks to embellish or exaggerate the severity of the collision, perhaps in a wholly genuine (but misguided) attempt to convince the Judge that the impact was significant enough to cause them genuine injury; perhaps in a wholly dishonest attempt to prove something the Claimant knows to be untrue. However, the photographic evidence and/or the engineering evidence may not, on its face, suggest a collision of any real force or seriousness. In some cases, the documentation shows damage which can only fairly be described as "light" or "minor". Where there is a stark contrast between the objective evidence as to the damage actually sustained, and the subjective reporting of the Claimant as to the magnitude of the collision, Claimants often find their case in a precarious position.

(c) The expert engineering evidence is unsatisfactory

In some instances, the expert evidence is simply not good enough and contains obvious logical or factual mistakes. In cases where the Claimant is a reasonably good witness, Courts tend to need very little persuading to disregard or give very little weight to an expert engineer's report which can be shown to be flawed in some way, notwithstanding its status as *expert* evidence.

CHAPTER EIGHT

CONCLUDING
OBSERVATIONS

Whilst low-velocity impact defences will by now be very familiar to anyone involved in road-traffic collision litigation, they are still not without their controversy or their difficulties. Notwithstanding advancements in medical and engineering understanding a fierce debate continues to rage as to whether, and if so in what circumstances, it can reliably be concluded that, by its very nature, a collision was *incapable* of causing bodily injury. There are still those who opine (with, it has to be accepted, some force) that there are far too many variables to be able to ever say that a collision was, by its nature, *incapable* of causing injury. It seems highly unlikely that a consensus will ever be reached in that respect and so the debate will continue.

The now longstanding guidance in *Kearsley* and *Casey* make clear how litigators on both sides of these cases should approach the issue of LVI. The guidance is tolerably clear; there is a focus on identifying the issue in early course and on providing relevant documentation voluntarily in an attempt to explore and, if possible, narrow the issues. Regrettably, experience suggests that the guidance is not always followed, or certainly not as closely as it ought to be. That may be a symptom of many LVI cases proceeding on the Fast Track where fixed costs arguably hamper a Claimant's ability to prepare his/her case as thoroughly or meticulously as he/she may like; as well as a symptom of Qualified-One Way Costs Shifting, meaning that Defendants generally have no prospect of recovering their costs, even where they are successful at trial, thereby arguably leading to the adoption of more costs efficient, but probably less thorough or compliant, approaches to the running of LVI defences. It is not difficult to be sympathetic with both positions, however neither is likely to be an argument which readily finds favour with the Court, and neither should be allowed to prevent compliance with the *Kearsley* and

Casey guidelines. Any failure to follow the Court of Appeal's guidance may have drastic consequences, particularly for Defendants, who may well lose the chance to run a LVI defence, at all.

It is regrettable that the series of test cases to be heard by a High Court Judge, as envisaged by the Court of Appeal, never materialised as that might have provided further welcome clarity on how such cases are to be prepared and tried. It seems unlikely such an exercise will now ever take place but that is perhaps a positive reflection on the Court's ability to deal with LVI defences in a broadly fair and consistent manner no matter where in England and Wales they are heard.

As this work has discussed, there are many sources of evidence and information which are relevant in LVI cases, and it is important that the evidence is collated and preserved timeously, irrespective of whether one is acting for the Claimant or Defendant. It is important to consider whether the evidence, as a whole, presents a (broadly) consistent account of the accident (including its nature and seriousness) and the injuries sustained, and whether that account is (broadly) commensurate with the objective evidence of damage. If the Claimant's account is lacking in one or more of those respects, it is imperative that his/her advisors ascertain why that is the case and deal with such inconsistencies in advance where possible as they will undoubtedly form a line of attack from the Defendant at trial.

The prospects of success of a LVI defence should be kept under constant review. There is often an evolving evidential landscape which requires an honest reappraisal when new evidence or information comes to light. Certainly, from a Defendant's perspective, there must be an objective and realistic assessment of the prospects of the defence in light of all the evidence. It is probably unwise to proceed to trial simply in the hope that the Claimant will be a poor witness, when the other objective evidence points in favour of the collision being more than a minor coming together of two vehicles.

The Claimant's medical records are likely to be highly important documents in a LVI case. They must be scrutinised carefully and any issues, particularly relating to consistency of reporting or failures to report relevant entries to the medico-legal expert(s), must be raised with the Claimant and instructions for the inconsistency taken. The Claimant may have perfectly legitimate explanations for the perceived failures in his/her reporting; he/she may also have no good answer at all.

Without doubt the key factor in most, if not all, LVI cases is the Claimant's credibility as a witness. The Claimant's advisors have an ability to assess this in conference long before the trial and they must take the opportunity to do so. Defendants, of course, are unable to assess the Claimant's credibility at any point prior to the trial itself but where the Defendant driver is to give his/her own evidence, the same considerations naturally apply.

Most cases are won, or lost, on the strength of the Claimant's own evidence and whether he/she is credible, or not. Expert medical or engineering evidence has a role (sometimes a very important role) to play in determining the outcome of a LVI case, but it is by no means guaranteed that expert evidence will be the deciding factor as regards the outcome at trial. Where the Claimant is impressive and the Court accepts his/her evidence as being truthful, such evidence may well be preferred even though the Defendant's expert evidence concludes no injury could have been sustained, has no logical flaws and withstands challenge.

Where expert evidence is deployed, particularly that of a forensic engineering expert, it is imperative that the material the expert relies upon to reach his/her conclusions is, itself, reliable and comprehensive. Where there are deficiencies in the underlying material these naturally permeate into the report itself. The quality of forensic engineering evidence varies quite significantly; it is extremely important that the content of the report is checked to ensure it is logical, coherent, appropriately reasoned, and the conclusions are supported by the underlying material and reasoning; the Court is unlikely to need much persuading to discount entirely, or attach very little weight to, a report that has demonstrable flaws, particularly where the Claimant is a credible and straightforward witness.

MORE BOOKS BY
LAW BRIEF PUBLISHING

A selection of our other titles available now:-

'A Practical Guide to Parental Alienation in Private and Public Law Children Cases' by Sam King QC & Frankie Shama
'Contested Heritage – Removing Art from Land and Historic Buildings' by Richard Harwood QC, Catherine Dobson, David Sawtell
'The Limits of Separate Legal Personality: When Those Running a Company Can Be Held Personally Liable for Losses Caused to Third Parties Outside of the Company' by Dr Mike Wilkinson
'A Practical Guide to Transgender Law' by Robin Moira White & Nicola Newbegin
'Artificial Intelligence – The Practical Legal Issues (2nd Edition)' by John Buyers
'A Practical Guide to Residential Freehold Conveyancing' by Lorraine Richardson
'A Practical Guide to Pensions on Divorce for Lawyers' by Bryan Scant
'A Practical Guide to Challenging Sham Marriage Allegations in Immigration Law' by Priya Solanki
'A Practical Guide to Legal Rights in Scotland' by Sarah-Jane Macdonald
'A Practical Guide to New Build Conveyancing' by Paul Sams & Rebecca East
'A Practical Guide to Defending Barristers in Disciplinary Cases' by Marc Beaumont
'A Practical Guide to Inherited Wealth on Divorce' by Hayley Trim
'A Practical Guide to Practice Direction 12J and Domestic Abuse in Private Law Children Proceedings' by Rebecca Cross & Malvika Jaganmohan
'A Practical Guide to Confiscation and Restraint' by Narita Bahra QC, John Carl Townsend, David Winch
'A Practical Guide to the Law of Forests in Scotland' by Philip Buchan
'A Practical Guide to Health and Medical Cases in Immigration Law' by Rebecca Chapman & Miranda Butler
'A Practical Guide to Bad Character Evidence for Criminal Practitioners by Aparna Rao
'A Practical Guide to Extradition Law post-Brexit' by Myles Grandison et al

'A Practical Guide to Equity Release for Advisors' by Paul Sams
'A Practical Guide to Financial Services Claims' by Chris Hegarty
'The Law of Houses in Multiple Occupation: A Practical Guide to HMO Proceedings' by Julian Hunt
'Occupiers, Highways and Defective Premises Claims: A Practical Guide Post-Jackson – 2nd Edition' by Andrew Mckie
'A Practical Guide to Financial Ombudsman Service Claims' by Adam Temple & Robert Scrivenor
'A Practical Guide to Advising Schools on Employment Law' by Jonathan Holden
'A Practical Guide to Running Housing Disrepair and Cavity Wall Claims: 2nd Edition' by Andrew Mckie & Ian Skeate
'A Practical Guide to Holiday Sickness Claims – 2nd Edition' by Andrew Mckie & Ian Skeate
'Arguments and Tactics for Personal Injury and Clinical Negligence Claims' by Dorian Williams
'A Practical Guide to Drone Law' by Rufus Ballaster, Andrew Firman, Eleanor Clot
'A Practical Guide to Compliance for Personal Injury Firms Working With Claims Management Companies' by Paul Bennett
'RTA Allegations of Fraud in a Post-Jackson Era: The Handbook – 2nd Edition' by Andrew Mckie
'RTA Personal Injury Claims: A Practical Guide Post-Jackson' by Andrew Mckie
'On Experts: CPR35 for Lawyers and Experts' by David Boyle
'An Introduction to Personal Injury Law' by David Boyle

These books and more are available to order online direct from the publisher at www.lawbriefpublishing.com, where you can also read free sample chapters. For any queries, contact us on 0844 587 2383 or mail@lawbriefpublishing.com.

Our books are also usually in stock at www.amazon.co.uk with free next day delivery for Prime members, and at good legal bookshops such as Wildy & Sons.

We are regularly launching new books in our series of practical day-to-day practitioners' guides. Visit our website and join our free newsletter to be kept informed and to receive special offers, free chapters, etc.

You can also follow us on Twitter at www.twitter.com/lawbriefpub.